About the Book

Julius Erving, popularly known as Dr. J, ranks as one of the most remarkable players in basketball today. His infectious urge to win and his incomparable moves combine for a memorable show of basketball wizardry that keeps the fans in the arena until the last minute of playing time. In this exciting biography, noted sportswriter Louis Sabin traces the career of Dr. J from the blacktop days of his childhood to his current position as forward for the New York Nets, and Sabin explains why everyone associated with basketball agrees that for total ability, pure excitement, and game-after-game inspiration, no other player compares to that magical super-superstar Dr. J.

by Louis Sabin

The Fabulous
DR. J
All-Time All-Star

G. P. Putnam's Sons, New York

Library of Congress Cataloging in Publication Data Sabin,
Louis The Fabulous Dr. J, All Time All Star. (Putnam
Sports Shelf) Includes index. Summary: A biography of
professional basketball player Julius Erving, known as Dr.
J., who plays for the New York Nets. 1. Erving, Julius—
Juvenile literature. 2. Basketball—Juvenile literature. [1.
Erving, Julius. 2 Basketball—Biography] I. Title. GV884.
E78S22 1976 796.32'3'0924 [B] [92] 76-23124

For my favorite teammates, Fran and Keith

Contents

The Fabulous Dr. J
All-Time All-Star

1

The Ghetto Game

The two boys stand facing each other, their eyes narrowed to slits. Their slim bodies are tense, and sweat streaks run in thin lines down their dark faces. The boy with the basketball wipes a ribbon of sweat from his forehead before it reaches his brow. The other boy, hunched forward, doesn't move. He keeps a steady gaze on his adversary and the basketball.

Now the one with the ball flashes a brief smile and begins to bounce the ball. The thump, thump, thump of the basketball makes a strangely hollow sound in the empty playground. The two boys are playing one-on-one early on a summer morning. It is a game between friends, yet they are as serious as if they were performing before thousands of fans in a professional arena.

The boy dribbling the ball switches it from left hand to right, at the same time dancing back a couple of steps to see what his opponent will do. The other boy's eyes stay with the ball, and he holds his ground. His refusal to budge is a clear declaration: "I'll give you the shot. Go on, take it. I don't think you can make it from that far out."

The dribbler is fifteen feet from the iron hoop. He

lowed by others as more boys filter down to the playground, taking turns at challenging the winner of each game. Julius is always the one who stays on the court. Finally, the boys choose sides for a game of three-on-three, and play doesn't slow until darkness comes. Then the playground attendant clears them out and locks the gate for the night.

The sky over Hempstead, Long Island, was cloudy; there were no stars or moon to light the ground below. It was 4 A.M., and the streets were early-morning silent. Then the quiet was broken by the squeak of a door opening and closing behind a young boy leaving a four-story project building. It was Julius, wearing the same sneakers he had worn on the playground court the day before, but there was no basketball in sight.

Whistling, as children sometimes do to comfort themselves in dark, lonely places, he moved along the street. In his arms were newspapers, and he walked from sidewalk to buildings, again and again, dropping papers in front of doors. As he went along his delivery route, his steps got springier, his whistle more cheerful. The night sky at last gave way to the first rays of light as dawn came to the poor neighborhood in this section of New York State.

By 8 A.M. the last of the papers were delivered, but his day was only beginning. Once he had dropped off the last newspaper, the hardworking ten-year-

knows he can take the open shot but isn't sure he can pop it in. Besides, the defender is daring him to come on: "If you won't shoot, see if you can drive past me, fake me out."

Their eyes lock again, for just a fraction of a section, but it is all the time needed for the boy with the ball. His feet shift swiftly; he takes a long, gliding first step and whips the ball between his legs and ahead of him. By the time the ball has passed from one hand to the other the offensive maneuver has confused the defender just enough to give the dribbler the advantage. Now he is skimming past the hand that reaches too late to grab the ball, and his body is launched into the air by the powerful thrust of right leg against the asphalt court. The defender stands by, momentarily frozen, helpless and angry at himself, as his opponent's hand cushions the ball until he reaches the peak of his jump, then snaps it up against the backboard. The ball angles off the board and drops through the metal ring.

"Nice shot, Julius," the beaten defender says grudgingly.

Julius grins, nods at the compliment, and starts to dribble the ball again. He has just begun to play; their game of one-on-one has a long way to go before one of them scores the 100 points that will decide the winner. He seems to be insisting, "What are you waiting for? We just started. Let's get it on!"

The game continues to its conclusion. It is fol-

old could turn his full attention to the subject that dominated his thoughts every day of the year: sports. And basketball, most of all.

After dashing home for breakfast, then grabbing his basketball, he was back on the street and hurrying to Campbell Park. That was where the basketball court was, where he could pour all his energy and enthusiasm into playing the game he loved. If he was alone, that meant time to practice dribbling, shooting, and rebounding, imagining opponents shadowing him and the ball each time he made a move.

He would dribble the ball cleverly, practicing things he had seen the older boys do, sometimes going up for a jump shot, sometimes sweeping past a phantom guard to drive for a two-point lay-up. Once in a while he would miss on purpose, so he could bound high into the air for the ball that caromed off the backboard. He'd snare it and immediately rocket into the air again, to toss the ball through the hoop.

Dribbling away from the backboard, he'd work around a perimeter, taking jump shots from ten to fifteen feet away. Or holding the ball and giving his "opponent" head and body fakes, he'd leap straight up and let loose a one-handed shot. Or he'd cut to his left or right, slam to a sudden stop, and rise into the air, releasing the ball at the peak of his leap.

Julius' friends would arrive sooner or later. That

was when the make-believe world became real. That was when the uncontested shots and shifty body movements were tested against other hope-filled young players, who tried to check and block and defeat the best inventions of Julius' court skills.

And it was there on the playground stage, where boys with visions of stardom acted out their scenes of conquest, that the basketball genius of Julius Erving really glowed. For the other boys, the brilliant plays and fantastic shots remained bottled up in their heads. For Julius, the fakes worked to perfection, the shots went in, the magic in his mind was successfully transformed to reality as he unveiled his latest tricks in those playground rivalries.

The other boys watched him and marveled at his grace and strength on the court. They tried to stop his newest inventions, tried to overpower him or out-duel him, but few ever came up with the right solutions. And while he put on his young version of the Julius Erving Show, a Campbell Park supervisor named Andy Haggerty studied his play and decided the youngster should be playing with an organized team on a regular basis. He knew of one team that was well run, had uniforms, and played an arranged schedule of games. It was part of the Hempstead Salvation Army community program and was coached by a friend of his, Don Ryan.

Julius was introduced to Ryan, and the man offered the boy the chance to join his team. Julius jumped at the offer. It was the beginning of a permanent friendship between a white man dedicated to helping boys through sports and a black boy who was dedicated to making something of his life through basketball and a sound education.

Playing for Don Ryan rewarded Julius both as a basketball player and as a person. When they weren't talking basketball, the subject Ryan emphasized was education. No matter how far he went as an athlete, Ryan pointed out, a person who took advantage of what school had to offer could look forward to a better, more satisfying life.

Julius listened and recognized the truth of what his coach was saying. He also listened well to the tips Ryan gave him about improving his game. They helped him to refine his already fast-developing skills, and it showed as Ryan's team marched through their basketball schedule.

At eleven, Julius was a five-foot-six-inch kangaroo who regularly outjumped opponents standing six or seven inches taller. He had extremely large hands for his age, which gave him gluelike control of the ball. He put these gifts to work for Ryan's well-balanced squad, which finished Julius' first season with a record of 27 wins and 3 losses. Julius improved steadily in his second year, and so did the team's won-lost figures as Ryan's boys took 31 games while losing only 1. He was just twelve, but the name of Julius Erving was spreading all over Long Island —and beyond.

Julius gave full credit to Don Ryan. He told a reporter a number of years later, "Don Ryan was very helpful to me in my view of life. You see, I grew up never knowing I was on the wrong side of the track. Then, when I started to look around me and see the way other people were living, I said to Don Ryan, 'What do I have to do to get like them?' And he told me, 'You have to perform in school the same as you do on the basketball court.' "

Julius followed Ryan's advice. That wasn't too hard since he had always been as serious-minded about his studies as he was about "studying" basketball. Still, he felt a gratitude for all the guidance and support Ryan gave him, and he later expressed that feeling by giving the coach a picture of himself with this inscription: "To Don, words can never say how much I admire you and your objectives. Nor can words say how much I appreciate what you've done for me personally."

In his typically modest way, Don Ryan refused credit for shaping the youngster whom he helped launch to basketball stardom. Instead, he said, "Julius' mother is the reason he did so well and was aways a good person." Ryan insisted that Mrs. Erving provided the basic ingredients as a model for the boy who left a warm bed at 4 A.M. to deliver newspapers every day. "He got it all from her," Ryan stated, and Julius built the rest of his life on that solid foundation.

Julius certainly agreed that his mother was one

in a million. From the day he was born on February 22, 1950, in Hempstead, he recalled, "We were very poor. My parents separated when I was three. My mother did domestic work, cleaning other people's houses. We lived in a project and received social services. My mother raised us—my sister, Alexis, my brother, Marvin, and me. And I really appreciated what she was doing all those years. She put food on the table. When I asked her for sneakers that were better, she got them. We didn't ask her for much, but if you wanted it, she got it."

With people like his mother and Don Ryan encouraging him, Julius was being gently led along a road that would one day lead him out of the world of welfare and playground courts to wealth, polished hardwood arena floors, and fame. And one day, when he looked back, he would see that others with whom he had grown up hadn't been so fortunate. Some of his childhood friends, taking a different route, would end up in trouble, in prison, on an endless treadmill to nowhere.

When he was thirteen, Julius' mother remarried, a man whose last name was Lindsay. About the same time the family moved a few miles away, to Roosevelt, Long Island. Although they had shifted from one poor neighborhood to another, Julius still had the necessities of his young life. Particularly a nearby basketball court. Roosevelt Park had a new one, painted green with white lines, with a basket at each end. The court, his imagination, and competition were all he needed.

"If somebody else was around," he remembered, "I'd play one-on-one, a hundred points wins. We didn't play for money. We played for ego, for pride."

When his time wasn't taken up by school and studying or by family responsibilities, Julius was free to plunge back into his precious universe of basketball. When he wasn't playing the game, he was watching it on television. And since he was a continuous learner, he put the information he gleaned from the televised games to work for him.

"I used to watch those games on television," he said. "My palms would sweat, and I'd think of moves no one else had done. I'd learn by watching good guys and bad guys. I'd dream up fantastic moves and then go out on the court and make them work." Then he paused, as if mentally re-creating those long-ago days on the Roosevelt Park court. "Some of those moves took a long time to develop," he concluded.

It was a long way from poverty to the pros, but Julius was making his plans to get from one to the other way back then. Even at thirteen he had his eyes on a promising horizon that, with work and dedication, would come closer every year.

2

Getting Better All the Time

Young Julius poured himself, body and brain, into basketball. Playing with Don Ryan's team, at games away from home, Julius learned something else about competition. He learned that there were other boys like him, in every part of America, who loved the sport and showed that love by spending morning-to-night hours playing it. Their heartfelt hopes of making a professional roster were the same as his— the hopes of children of poverty who glimpse a way out of the streets. And as Julius did in Roosevelt Park, those other young dreamers dribbled, re-bounded, and put the ball through hoops at local playgrounds in Los Angeles' Watts district, Cleve-land's Hough district, Brooklyn's Bedford-Stuyve-sant, Manhattan's Harlem . . . everywhere in Amer-ica where hopes can be built by a boy with a ball and a basket to shoot it at.

One of the places Julius learned about was Har-lem, a ghetto in upper Manhattan, New York. It is an area where black and Latin youngsters lead a harsh existence, a place where any kind of fun is welcome. Sport provides the best, the healthiest kind of fun. Give them a basketball or a baseball and a bat, and they can play and, while playing, forget the pain of family unemployment, the limited amount of food, the poor clothing, and all the other depressing realities of ghetto life.

Ghetto kids know there are better things in life, and one of the lessons they learn early is to be competitive. If you don't compete, you don't get your share. Winning really matters, and winning at anything becomes deeply important. They know they have to be competitive, or they are not going to be ready to meet the demands of the world waiting for them as adults.

"Pride" is a word that Julius Erving used to describe his motive to succeed as a young boy, and in every ghetto of American a boy's pride is often the only thing he has. Basketball, especially, is a game of pride. On the outdoor courts it is the half-court go-go-go of one-on-one or two-on-two, with loss of pride as the penalty for defeat. The winner walks around with his head held high. And if he takes two or three games in a row or really wipes out one of the other local stars, then his walk takes on a strut.

In time, when you get so good that your reputation spreads, other hotshot playground "kings" come looking for you. They want to take you on, like the Western gunslinger who had a reputation to build and went searching for the best "guns" around, so he could win recognition as the fastest gun in the territory.

That's the way it is in New York, where the basbetball replaces the six-gun and the shoot-out takes place on a court. And that's the way it became with Julius, when challengers starting coming around to meet and beat him, to add glory to their names. Beat another local teenage hero, and word of it flew along the grapevine that trails throughout every borough of New York, where many thousands of young basketball players swap stories of their personal playground heroes. They were wise to the fact that a big enough reputation catches the ears of adults who scout for colleges. And a scout's recommendation can lead to a scholarship, which can be followed by a national reputation. And *that* can take you right into the National Basketball Association or the American Basketball Association.

It happened to Walt Frazier and Billy Cunningham and a lot of other kids, didn't it? Well, man, that's the biggest basketball move of all—out of the ghetto, a reach-for-the-sky leap away from the curses of poverty and poor education, the twin set of chains ghetto kids try to break.

That was in Julius' mind, day and night, in school, at home, on the basketball court. And while he was a good son and a fine student, it was with a basketball that he continued to shine the brightest. That was where Julius was at in 1964, when he tried out for the freshman team at Roosevelt Junior High. His talent was recognized instantly.

The basketball coach at Roosevelt Junior High School, Early Moseley, encouraged Julius to make full use of his special abilities. Moseley also spoke to Julius' mother, explaining that the time Julius would be spending in school, after classes were over, would not be a punishment for bad behavior or because he needed extra work in any subjects. He told Mrs. Lindsay that her son had unlimited potential as a basketball player.

"He'll be playing with the school team," Moseley said. "He'll do a lot for us, and we hope we can help him become an even better player than he is now."

Both Julius and his mother were pleased with the results of those after-school sessions. So was Moseley, whose team had an easy time against most opponents. At thirteen Julius still had his share of rough edges that had to be smoothed and rounded, but his superiority to other players was obvious. Athletically gifted, mature, and a quick learner, he was like an A student in a class of C students. The rough edges disappeared amazingly fast as he tried, and succeeded at, picking up the concepts of team play, moving without the ball, setting picks, and passing off to teammates in better scoring positions than he was. And every now and then he'd dip into his bag of playground tricks and startle everybody with an inventive move that most of them couldn't even imagine. Moseley would caution Julius to control his skillful exuberance but would smile to himself at the boy's brilliance.

By the time Julius was fourteen, the coach of the Roosevelt High School basketball team, Ray Wilson, was anxious to add Julius' name to the junior varsity roster. Coach Moseley, of course, didn't want to let him go since Julius' leadership guaranteed his junior high school squad another fine season. But Moseley wisely admitted that Julius was already better than most of the high school's varsity players, and he agreed that moving up to the junior varsity would be in Julius' best interests. There he would develop faster and be competing against more challenging players.

Wilson kept Julius on the junior varsity most of the season, letting the ninth grader sharpen his skills and his sense of team play. Then, with two contests left on the varsity schedule, the Roosevelt coach brought Julius up to the "big" team.

Julius worked out with his new teammates, getting acquainted with their styles and the various plays favored by Coach Wilson. Now close to six feet in height, Julius was used at both guard and center. He didn't merely fit into the play of the older, more experienced varsity members, but stood out as far above them as an oak among birches.

However, Wilson preferred to let him ride the

bench throughout Roosevelt High's next-to-last game. He told Julius to be patient, to watch and learn. "Your chance will come," the coach assured him. Then, with only a few minutes remaining in the last game of the season, Wilson called out, "Okay, get in there and see what you can do."

Julius bounced onto the court and promptly went to work on the player guarding him. As one of the Roosevelt guards brought the ball across the mid-court line, Julius, assigned the low post position, lost his defender on a nifty fake-and-roll that took him near the basket. His guard's pass slapped into his hands; he dribbled under the basket and glided into the air. No one was near him as he released the ball with a slight flip of the wrist, and it settled into the cords.

The next year witnessed Julius' emergence as Roosevelt High's top player. Everyone who followed his career at the school *knew* he was the cream of the team, but Coach Wilson refused to start him. It was Wilson's belief that players who had been with the team all along had earned the right to start, and that was usually reserved for seniors. The juniors and sophomores would get their opportunity when they reached that grade.

However, the coach's rule didn't mean that only seniors would play—just that they would start. He knew what Julius could do and didn't keep him on the bench too long. He'd open a game with his five seniors, then bring in Julius as soon as his squad needed a jolt of playmaking, rebounding, or scoring.

Roosevelt High enjoyed a fine year, closing with 13 wins against 4 losses. Julius, now six feet two inches tall, had some other figures of which he was proud. He may not have started the games, but he certainly made up for lost time once he joined the action. He was Roosevelt's scoring king, with an average of 18 points a game, and its ace rebounder, too.

The high school standout looked back on his junior season as an important one. He had learned a great deal about full-court refereed games and about himsef as a player. "I was a good, but not great high school basketball player until my junior year," he observed sometime later. "Scholastically, I was ahead of my physical self. In my junior year I gave up all other sports and played basketball because I really dug it and saw it as a means to an end —going to college."

This studious, single-minded approach to basketball paid rich dividends during the summer between Julius' junior and senior years at Roosevelt High. His game shifted out of the gymnasium and back onto the playgrounds, where he applied the new ideas he had picked up in school competition, along with those he had seen on television and the ones he cooked up in his own creative brain.

He was also growing rapidly in height and adding weight and muscle to his finely tuned body. As soon as the summer "season" got under way, it was clear that he was miles ahead of the other players at Roosevelt Park. Then, unexpectedly, he encountered some excellent local competition. It came from a pair of teenagers who had moved into the neighborhood from other sections of the metropolitan area. They were six-foot-six-inch George Green and six-foot-three-inch Tommy Taylor, both a year behind Julius in school but almost at his level on a basketball court. Green was a hard-to-stop shooter, while Taylor made up for certain shortcomings by hustling every step of the way.

After a few playground matches against Julius, in which he really impressed them, Green and Taylor told him he just *had* to "go where the action is," to meet the top talent around the rest of the city. Julius had heard about the excellent brand of basketball being played in other parts of New York, and the idea appealed to him.

Green and Taylor took him to playgrounds in Brooklyn and Queens, where he pitted himself against "the dudes with the tough reps." Julius came off very well in those one-on-one contests, winning far more than he lost. Before long his name was being woven into the legendary history that was passed along the basketball grapevine. That naturally led to a parade of playground "gunslingers" finding their way to Julius' home court. They came looking to collect the scalp of the fabulous Julius Erving but usually went back to their own neighborhood after leaving their own scalps hanging from his belt.

Before the summer ended, Julius had inched up to six feet four inches and added a nickname to go with his city-wide reputation. His explanation of how he became the one and only "Dr. J" went this way: "In high school one fellow called himself the Professor and I called myself the Doctor. That was because I was thinking of becoming a doctor someday. Then, when I was playing pro ball in Virginia, teammate Willie Sojourner helped me make it into 'Doctor J.'"

The moves, the slick tricks, the skills Julius put on display at home and away became the models which younger New York players tried to copy. These imitators found it was far easier to describe than actually do them, because his dynamic actions required split-second decisions, razor-sharp reflexes, and superb physical equipment.

The incomparable teenager put on a memorable show of basketball wizardry, using every weapon available in his huge and ever-expanding store of moves. For example, there were the stuff shot, the dunk, and the slam-dunk. One time he might feel that all he had to do was take the easy route: take an effortless hop up, from directly beneath the backboard, and gently deposit the ball in the hoop. That was sometimes called the Doctor's Dunk. It sounded simple, but it wasn't. The way Julius reached the point where the gentle dunk took place, getting there was all the fun—and achievement—for it meant that he had to outplay a tenacious defender who was dead set against the Doctor making a fool of him.

Then there was the mind-blowing slam-dunk, which was executed with surgical precision as Julius one-handed the ball over the rim and whammed it through the netting.

Julius was especially fond of two other varieties: the hoop vibrating reverse stuff shot that drove his schoolyard fans wild and the behind-the-head stuff shot he loved to exhibit. The behind-the-head beauty left the crowd gasping and psychologically crushed the player who was the victim of this spectacular move. As he buried the ball in the netting, Julius' back would be to the basket, and he'd be grinning into the glazed eyes of his opponent.

Playground basbetball—a matter of pride and ego. And the stuff was the greatest ego play of all.

As the Doctor analyzed those high points of his schoolyard dunking days, he said, "There's a whole psychology there that makes you want to beat a guy in a way that makes him pay twice. You want to outscore him, and you also want to freak him out with a big move or a big block. That way, even if the score is tied, you and he both know you're really ahead."

Also, being six-foot-four-inches made Julius feel short when he came up against players standing anywhere from two to eight inches taller. But he had the answer to that problem. "I always had big hands and could jump," he said, "so I learned to be trickier than the bigger guys. I liked to experiment."

3

The Next Big Step

With the end of summer came the end of most of Julius' experimenting. It was back to school and Roosevelt High's basketball team. "Team" was the key word, because it meant individual players working together, and freewheeling talents had to be shaped to coincide with the needs of the five-man concept of cooperation. Without that, no team can win many games.

Coach Wilson had the players' cooperation. With George Green and Tommy Taylor joining him on the varsity, Julius felt the winter season was, in some ways, a continuation of the summer. They felt the same way, and they blended together swiftly, knowing the others' styles, able to anticipate what their teammates' thoughts and actions would be.

It proved to be a success-filled season for Coach Wilson's squad, victorious in 16 of 18 games. Julius averaged better than 20 points a game, but those two losses hurt. One of them had been to Roosevelt's archrival, Hempstead High, and the chance for revenge came in the second-regular-season meeting of the two teams.

With Julius pumping in 22 points and gathering 17 rebounds, Roosevelt earned that revenge by a score of 78 to 70. Now each team had a win over the other, and there was only one way to determine which was the better squad—a third contest. The only way that could happen was if they met in the county play-offs, and Julius could think of nothing he wanted more than for that confrontation to take place in the championship round.

In the first round Julius dominated the show by snaring 11 rebounds and notching 28 points, leading his team to a 82–48 thrashing of West Hempstead High. But the showdown between Roosevelt and Hempstead High didn't take place because Coach Wilson's boys were stopped in the second round, 62–49, even though Julius went all out with 19 points, strong boardwork, and fine teamplay.

"That game really disillusioned me," Julius said afterward, registering one of his rare complaints. "We were the black team [Elmont Memorial, a team composed of a predominantly white team, won the game], and there weren't too many others on Long Island. I sincerely believe we suffered at the hands of the refs because of that."

The lost opportunity to be a member of a championship team was a serious disappointment to the graduating senior. But Julius could console himself with the knowledge that quite a few colleges were ready to offer him scholarships to play basketball for them. His past was already bursting with glory and success, and his future promised more of the same. However, he realized the choice he made would be an extremely meaningful factor in just how bright that future would be. Nevertheless, he also knew he was facing a very welcome problem in having to decide which college would be most suitable for him.

Julius visited a number of colleges. Among them was the University of Iowa, which had been attended by another legendary New York area schoolyard "giant," Connie Hawkins. Hawkins had gone on to a noteworthy career in the ABA and the NBA, and Iowa would have been overjoyed to have had Julius add his name to their basketball history.

But Julius decided to concentrate on colleges closer to home. He wanted to be able to be nearby if his mother needed him. Julius' brother, Marvin, was suffering from a rare disease that eventually took his life at the age of sixteen, and his sister, Alexis, was preparing to marry and move out of town.

Julius' loyalty to his mother, who had done so much for him over the years, was an important factor in his choice of college. So was the warm relationship that had developed between him and the three coaches who had contributed so much to his growth as a player and person—Don Ryan, Earl Moseley, and Ray Wilson.

So, even though he visited Iowa, he was really

zeroing in on Eastern colleges, such as Penn State, St. John's, Manhattan, Hofstra, Boston University, and the University of Massachusetts.

Ray Wilson was always available to assist Julius in weighing the merits of the different schools, to figure out the positive and negative qualities of each one in terms of Julius' well-being and future. Wilson knew how critical it was for Julius to pick the right college because, the coach said, "So many kids go away to college as major talents and become monsters. The only thing a coach can hope for is that they'll treat your kid like a man. You don't ask for any favors. You just want him to get a chance to play and learn. So your best bet is to guide him somewhere you know the coach."

One coach Wilson knew well was Jack Leaman, with whom he had played college ball. Leaman was the head coach at the University of Massachusetts. UMass had a good reputation for its educational program and was set out in the countryside of New England. It was a place where there wouldn't be too many undesirable distractions for a student intent on learning rather than on having a "fun" time.

The fact that the school didn't have a high-pressure big-name sports-conscious attitude didn't bother Julius. In fact, that was part of what he was seeking as he weighed one college against another. At last, after much thought and discussion, Julius chose UMass.

"I prefer the campus life," he said. "I want to find out about the New England way of life and what it's like in the country. The overall picture at Massachusetts appealed to me."

Also appealing to him was the feeling that the school's student body and teaching staff would think of him as a person, not just a jock. "I feel Massachusetts is right for me," Julius said, "because it isn't a meat-grinder school, where they just use your body. The UMass coach, Jack Leaman, was concerned about *me*."

This decision pleased everyone who cared about Julius the man, not only Julius the basketball player. Ray Wilson, who would join Julius at UMass in 1969 as the assistant basketball coach, received the news of Julius' choice with the kind of smile that a father would wear upon hearing that his son had performed some marvelous deed.

Julius entered the campus world in the fall of 1968. He immediately settled into the life of the freshman, taking advantage of the education that was being offered to him. But he wasn't the kind of student some people mock as "a total grind." When he wasn't spending hours with his books, he was practicing his basketball skills. And as a student will concentrate on his weakness in a particular class, Julius concentrated on his weakness on the court. That weakness was his outside shooting.

Anyone wandering into the Boyden Building, the

men's physical education center, that September was sure to see a young man— six foot four inches tall, muscular and agile—focusing his mind and body on the art of putting a round ball through an iron ring. One UMass student who discovered Julius practicing all by himself described it this way: "He was wearing just a pair of shorts, because it was really warm in the center. His body was shiny with sweat, but he didn't seem to notice the heat. He also didn't seem to notice anybody or anything else. His mind was fixed on the ball and the basket.

"Some of the other guys saw him working out by himself, and they passed the word around that he was something else, the kind of player you just don't see around a place like UMass. Well, before long the bleachers were filled with kids sitting and really digging him doing his thing.

"What he did wasn't what you'd call spectacular. He'd just work his way around the floor in a half circle about fifteen to eighteen feet from the basket, throwing up shot after shot. Every once in a while he'd go up for a lay-up, to break the monotony, I guess. Like I said, he didn't do anything spectacular, yet you had to be impressed by his single-minded dedication and the fantastic way he moved."

At first, the UMass kids were just curious about a player who would give so much time to practicing the same kind of shot. "But it didn't take long for Erving's day-after-day workout to get to the people who dropped by," said the student. "It was like watching a scientist doing some experiment, doing it over and over, sure he'd find what he was looking for if he just stayed with it. That's what sort of hypnotized us, and it caused a sort of electricity to come over everybody in those bleacher seats. UMass isn't what you'd call a magnet for superathletes, and nobody thinks about our teams' chances in the Yankee Conference no matter what sport you're talking about. But Erving's nonstop practicing and his reputation really jolted our interest in the basketball team."

That interest picked up as the students came to see Julius and the rest of the freshman team start practice in October. Julius's improved accuracy from fifteen to eighteen feet, plus his quick moves and inventive playmaking, led the freshman coach, Pete Broker, to play him as much at guard as at forward. But it didn't take long for Broker and varsity Coach Leaman to recognize that Julius' rebounding value was being wasted when he was used as a guard. Soon he was solidly entrenched at forward, made the focus of the team's offense, and set plays were devised to suit his special talents.

The freshman team opened the season with a couple of wins, and the student body began pouring into the Curry Hicks Cage to witness the kind of basketball that was common at UCLA but as rare as diamonds at UMass. And with Julius playing his brand of ball, breaking the school's freshman records for rebounding and scoring, Coach Broker's boys ripped through an untouchable season, winning 16 and losing none. That red-hot basketball inspired the varsity, which put together *its* best season, winning 18 games while losing only 6.

Julius was unquestionably the big man on campus. Everybody was basketball-conscious now. For the first time in the school's history there was talk about the possibility of the UMass Redmen being invited to a major tournament the next year, when Julius moved up to the varsity. Julius took it all in stride, enjoying the success but not overemphasizing it. He kept a level head, went to classes, studied, and gave as much energy and time to his books as he did to his sport. He didn't want to complete college as an overdeveloped athlete with an underdeveloped brain.

That summer Julius was hired by the town of Hempstead as a supervisor at Roosevelt Park. Not only did it provide him the opportunity to earn some money and help out the kids who looked to him for guidance, as well as basketball instruction, but it also allowed him the freedom to practice. As soon as the playground was officially closed, he would take to the court and practice the way he had all through his childhood. Only now he had a much clearer idea of what parts of his game needed the most attention, and he didn't waste time with meaningless dunks.

He was nearer his dream of one day being drafted by a professional team, and he knew that kind of dream wouldn't come true without his helping it along.

The fall of 1969 brought Julius back to the campus for his sophomore year. Arriving at the same time, as assistant varsity coach, was Ray Wilson, his Roosevelt High coach and good friend. It boosted Julius' already soaring spirits to have two coaches he liked and respected, a feeling that was shared by Wilson and Jack Leaman, and it promised to be a fine season.

The basketball season opened with less than the expected bang. The team split its first 12 games, and it seemed that the Redmen weren't going to live up to their high expectations. But then the players became accustomed to one another's styles, the coaches emphasized the strengths and strengthened the weaknesses, and the squad jelled with startling suddenness. When Julius found himself, it brought the team to life. After that, Leaman's boys went on a tear, taking 13 games in a row.

The Redmen wrapped up the regular season with 18 wins and 7 losses. The squad's big gun was, of course, Dr. J. He averaged 25.7 points a game, and his 20.1 rebounds per game ranked him second in the entire United States. The "anonymous" school, where academics came first and athletics second, was catapulted onto the national scene. Having won the rating as No. 1 college in all New England, UMass was offered a spot in the National Invitation Tournament (NIT) at New York's Madison Square Garden.

The idea of going back to "his town" as the leader of one of the nation's select teams gave Julius a special glow of pride. But the team's hopes looked gloomy when it was matched in the first round with the top-seeded team, Marquette University.

The game was a squeaker from the first seconds right down to the closing minutes. Julius, aching for a Madison Square Garden upset, gave it his best try. Marquette's talent-rich squad finally inched ahead, however, and edged UMass by 5 points.

Even though the defeat was disappointing, Coach Leaman's players had the satisfaction of knowing they had been beaten by the best. Marquette kept on winning to capture the NIT championship.

"They know we're around now," said one of Julius' teammates. "Until this tournament nobody paid much attention to a team that scheduled games against schools like Bates, Colby, and Amherst. But with Julius putting on his show, we came out of nowhere and stirred up some real interest. I mean, you got to admit that playing Marquette so tough didn't do our rep any harm, right?"

Right!

The season seemed over for Julius. After finishing

up his sophomore year at school, he took off for Indiana, where he had a job as a teacher at an instructional camp. However, one day he was notified that a squad of America's best college players—the U.S. Olympic Development Team—was being sent on a tour of Europe, and the organizers wanted him to play on it. He packed his bags and joined the team in Colorado within twelve hours.

What followed was a great deal of fine basketball with the additional reward of travel. Julius got to play alongside other pro-class basketball players and toured such countries as Finland, Poland, and the Soviet Union. Then, to add icing to the cake, he was named the most valuable player on the tour. This prompted one sportswriter to observe. "Lots of basketball-wise experts overlooked Julius Erving when it came to voting for this year's All-America team. Now I wonder how wise they think they really are."

Coach Leaman agreed, saying, "That showed Julius that, no matter how much recognition our school had or didn't have, he was as great as any college player in the country."

4

In a Class with the Pros

Dr. J was on his way. His confidence growing with success and recognition and his skills growing with a constant diet of basketball, Julius sailed into his junior year at UMass as one of America's finest professional prospects. The Redmen from Massachusetts were now being touted as a team to be reckoned with, and they owed it all to Dr. J, who had led them through the wall of obscurity that had surrounded them for years.

Coach Leaman was fully conscious of what Julius had done for his team and of what he could do in the upcoming season. So he did what every smart coach does with a star—he developed and put into practice court strategies that had the other players orbiting around Julius. It was a formula that assured UMass' dominance in the Yankee Conference and maybe something more in postseason tournament play.

The Redmen launched into the 1970–71 schedule like a skyrocket, with the Doctor an improved version of the dazzling court demon of the previous year. He was everywhere, doing everything, a gliding ghost that awed fans and foes alike as he appeared from nowhere to block shots and break up rival plays that seemed certain to succeed. Before long his reputation alone was enough to destroy an opposing team's composure.

He couldn't dunk—the college rule against dunking prohibited that. But his huge, iron-fingered hands and gazelle-high leaps assured him control of rebounds at both ends of the floor. So it came as no surprise that by midseason he was a national leader in rebounds, averaging close to 20 a game. As for scoring, his fancy fakes and drives to the basket drove fans wild and opponents crazy. Working inside, within ten feet of the backboard, he was the uncontested master, and he was averaging better than 27 points a game before the schedule was half over.

In the Redmen's first 14 contests they came out victorious 12 times. Only 2 losses—each one by the slimmest possible margin of 1 point—marred a perfect record. The students, tasting fame for the first time, were in a basketball frenzy, turned on to the team's every action by the superstar displays of their fantastic Dr. J.

Joining the UMass students in praise and admiration, but evaluating Julius with a much keener eye, was Assistant Coach Ray Wilson. As astounding as Julius was, Wilson said, "I have to believe he is going to get much better, too. Each time I see him he does something I've never seen him do before."

Never satisfied, Julius was creating new moves, refining old ones. All this moved Wilson to remark, "I watch television and I see Sidney Wicks, of UCLA, who's very quick and goes to the offensive boards. Well, so does Julius. Then I think, maybe Julius can shoot from deeper positions. All of a sudden, I sit back and say to myself, 'Am I talking about this class of ballplayer?' And the answer is yes."

Julius was also watching players like Wicks and other collegiate basketball stars who bore the stamp of the surefire professionals of tomorrow. He measured himself against them and, although still modest, had to feel honestly that he was at least equal to, if not better than, they.

And Julius was aware of the almost unbelievable sums of money being showered by the professional leagues on college players performing at that level. Some of those young men hadn't even completed their four years of college before being snapped up by the pros.

One was Ralph Simpson, a University of Michigan standout, who signed a contract to play for the ABA's Denver Rockets after his sophomore season at Michigan. Simpson's campus-to-pro-arena jump was brought about by a tempting offer of a three-year salary of $750,000 and a lifetime of financial security.

Another widely publicized college player to desert

the campus ranks for the ABA was Spencer Haywood. A University of Detroit undergraduate, Haywood agreed to play for pay—to the tune of $1,500,000 over six years—for the same Denver Rockets. But after spending a year with the ABA club, he was enticed to join the NBA's Seattle SuperSonics for an even juicier deal.

The message was clear to Julius: Haywood and Simpson flew from their campuses to the pros because they were motivated by two things—top-level competition and money . . . lots of it.

Julius certainly had nothing against earning the kind of salaries enjoyed by Simpson, Haywood, and others like them. However, he reminded himself of the education he was getting at UMass and the pleasure of playing for Leaman—and these things were also important to him. So even as he whirled through his triumphal junior season, he was nagged by the question of whether he should finish college or take the professional plunge.

It was a question that Ray Wilson was also considering. While he wanted Julius to continue to spearhead the UMass squad, he acknowledged that playing in the major leagues of basketball had to be a strong temptation even for someone as levelheaded as Julius. Wilson studied Dr. J as the season moved along and wondered if the young man—now six feet six and a half inches tall and blessed with all the tools of greatness—would find the lure of professional fame and money more than he could withstand. The coach suspected it wouldn't be too long before he'd find out.

It was still a few weeks before the end of Julius' junior year at UMass when he answered that question. "I feel I'm a more complete player now," he said. "I wasn't a natural shooter, and it was something I had to work on. I don't place any limitations on myself. When I began to grow and develop, I started to think seriously about pro ball."

Then he paused, his expression typically serious and thoughtful, before continuing. "But not even pro ball is the beginning and end of everything in a man's life. You can't play basketball all your life," he said. "Otherwise, why pursue a degree? Basketball is fun, but you've got to work, too. I've set a list of priorities already. First is studying, then playing ball as best I can. Everything else comes after."

On hearing this, Wilson observed, "Julius has always been realistic. He has direction. He knows where he wants to go. He sees pro ball as a possibility, but he's not basing his whole life on that. He's never lost sight of his goals. I think he works as hard on his studies as he does on his basketball."

Julius nodded his agreement, then added, "Between eighteen and twenty-two you develop in so many ways. You come in contact with all types of students—radicals of every sort. And there's something to be learned from them. I'm finding time for more things than basketball. You go to college only once."

That seemed to settle the matter of Dr. J's immediate plans, and he turned his attention back to the rest of the season. It was more of what the first half had been. With the Doctor's scoring and rebounding as its backbone, the UMass five rattled off eight more wins, upping their record to 20 victories against 2 losses. Then they swept into Madison Square Garden for a game against George Washington University.

On home ground again, with basketball-wise New York fans cheering in the stands, Julius cut loose with a barrage of attacking manuevers that swamped the GWU defenders trying to stop him. Notching 35 points and 17 rebounds, he lifted the Redmen to their twenty-first win and practically assured the team another shot at the NIT crown.

Julius ended the year with an average of 27 points a game, well up among the nation's best, and again took national rebounding honors on the strength of 19 caroms per game. At the same time the UMass Redmen wrapped up their regular schedule with a 23-3 record and a bid to return to Madison Square Garden for the 1971 National Invitation Tournament. This time they got past the first round, but that victory was their last of the season. As it had been the year before, the schedule was not in their favor. They were slated to meet top-seeded North Carolina in the second round. Not even Julius could produce the miracle UMass needed; NC was simply too much for the New England squad, crushing them by a 41-point margin.

Leaman and his team left New York as quickly as possible.

While Julius was licking his wounds from the bombing at the hands of North Carolina, his future was being discussed by some very influential people in the ABA. At this point in the battle for the best college talent, the NBA prohibited the drafting of any undergraduate until he had fulfilled his college obligations. The ABA, however, was struggling to catch up with the NBA, and the team owners were divided on the issue. Some believed all was fair in basketball and war, while others felt the same way as the NBA about keeping hands off until a player was out of college.

One ABA owner who wanted to draft Julius right away was Earl Foreman, owner of the Virginia Squires. Ray Boe, boss of the New York Nets, would have liked to add Julius to his roster. He knew that Dr. J had grown up practically in the shadow of the Nets' arena. But Boe was opposed to signing young men still in school. So Foreman was given the all clear to go after the UMass star. A short while later Julius was asked if he was ready to follow the examples of Ralph Simpson and Spencer Haywood.

It was really a dilemma for Julius. Before this

time he had talked about the possibility of playing in the pros as just that—a possibility. Now he was face to face with the reality, and it released emotions he hadn't had to deal with before.

Julius talked over the situation with people close to him. On the one hand, he was only a year away from acquiring something he had wanted and worked for since childhood: a degree from a good college. He knew that he, like Kareem Abdul-Jabbar, Bill Bradley, Jerry Lucas, and so many others who had earned degrees before starting their professional careers, wanted to develop his brain as well as his body.

On the other hand, Julius considered the possible dangers of waiting too long. There was the chance that the interleague bidding war might end at any time, especially if the NBA and ABA joined to make one professional league. Also, he might injure himself during his senior year with the UMass varsity. And always in his mind was the thought that he could give his mother the financial help she needed a year earlier simply by signing a Squires' contract offering him $500,000 over a four-year period.

Julius valued education highly, but it must have seemed like a luxury when he remembered the many hours he had spent earning pennies by delivering newspapers. And, of course, burned into his memory were the years his family had been on welfare.

After a difficult debate with himself Julius finally

decided to go professional. But before agreeing to the Virginia offer, he visited the offices of the New York Nets. There he spoke with the team's coach and general manager, Lou Carnesecca. Carnesecca had been the basketball coach at St. John's University when Julius chose to attend UMass rather than St. John's and a number of other colleges. Carnesecca had wanted Julius then, and he wanted him now, especially since the Doctor had proven he had the special gifts of a superstar.

Julius made it clear that he preferred to play for the team located in his home area, and Carnesecca was anxious to get him into a Nets' uniform. But when Carnesecca telephoned Ray Boe and told him Julius was right there, ready and available, Boe refused to break his rule about signing an underclassman. Boe knew as well as Carnesecca that another team's owner wouldn't hesitate at grabbing Julius— players like that drew fans and dollars by the thousands. But the Nets' owner sincerely felt that there were things more important than getting a player by any means.

And so, on April 6, 1971, Julius sat down to talk business with Earl Foreman. Accompanying Julius were Ray Wilson and Bob Woolf, a lawyer who had represented many athletes in their dealings with professional team owners. When the negotiations had ended, Julius was a Squire, Ray Wilson was happy for the young man he had grown so close to over the years, and—back in Massachusetts—Coach Jack Leaman had to resign himself to the fact that his Redmen would be a far different team without Julius. Still, the UMass coach conceded that Julius had made the most rational choice open to him.

The last words on the subject came from Julius' mother. After learning of her son's signing to play pro basketball, Mrs. Erving said, "Julius was never a snappy child. He always liked to listen, and he didn't give anyone cause to dislike him. He is smart and deep-thinking. It's wonderful how he made it up to the pros. He's a good boy and I'm happy for him. When he graduated from high school, he said to me, 'This is the beginning. I mean to go far.' I guess he thought that out like everything else."

Now Julius turned his thoughts to the ABA. It was another beginning for him, and there was no doubt in his mind that he again meant to go far.

5

Running Wild

The red-white-and-blue basketball left the fingers of the shooter, flew in almost a straight line, and skipped off the rim of the hoop. It banged sharply against the backboard and angled upward. Instantly, Virginia Squires rookies converged on the ball, a flury of shoving, elbowing players staking out territory to snare the carom.

Fire blazed in their eyes, and fury was unleashed in the savage movements of their sinewy arms and legs. This was no college game, where players competed for the applause of schoolmates and a pat on the back from the coach. Nor was it a schoolyard scramble, one of those three-on-three pickup contests that combine showboating and fun and ego satisfaction. This was serious basketball, as serious as the game could get. It was the rookie camp of a professional team, where each man was working—working, not just playing—to prove he had the guts, the talent, and the drive to earn a place on the roster. If he didn't make it here, he stood a good chance of ending up on some foreign team or in one of America's minor leagues, struggling for another shot at the big time. Fail now and his description would be: *Almost* good enough for the pros, but he flunked the crucial test.

The bruising contact under the backboard grew in intensity. Standing on the sideline, studying the action and gauging each rookie, was Squires' Coach Al Bianchi. An ex-NBA guard, Bianchi had endured this kind of battle for survival, and he knew what these players were thinking and feeling.

Right now the candidates were grunting from the body-to-body effort, grinding and bumping shoulders and hips, straining every muscle in their effort to capture the descending ball. Suddenly, even as their hands stretched up and their legs pistoned them into the air around the basket, a body took off from the floor eight feet from that boiling mass of ball-hungry rookies.

Bianchi's gaze flicked to the flying form, his eyes widening as it went up and, like a bird whose wings have caught the wind, rose still higher as it swooped toward the rebound. At that instant the scene seemed to freeze—the players locked in place as if a photographer had ordered them to "Hold it!"

Then the action resumed as the swooping rebounder extended a long arm, opened wide the huge hand at the end of that arm, and claimed the ball in an unbreakable grip. The player's sneakers slammed to the floor, the ball squeezed between those huge hands, and the other rookies just stared at him with frustration and admiration.

The player was, of course, Julius Erving. There was really no need for him to go all out to win a place on the team. He was *the* rookie, the half-million-dollar prize, and no one actually expected him to risk injuring himself in these workouts. But the man with the No. 32 jersey didn't see it that way. He had come to play, and he knew only one way of playing—hard and with the exciting flair for the spectacular that had been his trademark from his early days on playground courts.

The competitor in Dr. J was always in evidence. And the aggressiveness of the other rookies added fuel to Julius's normally pride-driven desire to excel. One of the newcomers was six-foot eight-inch Willie Sojourner. A seven-foot high jumper in college, Sojourner was in contention for the center position; but he was also a promising candidate for a forward slot, and that put him in Julius' territory. They were good friends, but both understood that the bonds of friendship aren't strong when the ball is in play.

Another factor motivating Julius' efforts was his craving to help make Virginia a winning team. The Squires' owner, Earl Foreman, was pushing for more interleague play between the ABA and the NBA. He wanted the ABA to improve to the point at which the NBA would have to admit that it was no longer superior to the younger league. Foreman was convinced that the way to build the ABA was to sign as many top college stars as possibe and to lure big-name NBA players into the ABA. And he believed that the logical place to start his campaign for equality was in Virginia, by shaping his Squires into a great team.

After signing Erving and Sojourner, Foreman declared, "I don't want to make the Virginia team just the best in the ABA. I want to make it the best in all of professional basketball."

That was the kind of thinking that made sense to Julius, and even though he could have eased up a little in those preseason workouts, he turned in the brand of basketball that merited the description, "the best."

Yet while Julius was impressing the Squires' management right from the first day of camp, he also was giving them reason to worry. On that first day the team's general manager, Johnny Kerr, expressed his concern about the Doctor's daring, bone-jarring moves around the backboard. A former NBA center, Kerr had seen more than one player break bones and tear muscles in the unrestrained melees of preseason practice. Remembering that, he didn't want to see this valuable young man sidelined by injury at any time—and certainly not as a result of some freak accident during rookie workouts.

After witnessing Julius' flying rebound, Kerr told Coach Bianchi, "Sure, he looked fantastic, but you'd better get him out of there. You don't want him to hurt himself."

Bianchi appreciated Kerr's concern, but he was also deeply impressed by Julius' hustle and seemingly unlimited energy. "He'll be all right," Bianchi answered. "In fact, I'm sure he'll be more than all right. He may be a rookie, but I'm counting on him to play forty minutes a game for us, right from the start."

Bianchi's faith in Julius was so complete that one of the team's starting forwards, George Carter, was traded to the Pittsburgh Condors a few days later. Carter had been a 19-points-a-game scorer for the Squires the previous season, in which they had won 55 games, while losing 29, to capture the Eastern Division title.

If the Virginia management and players were impressed by Julius, he was equally impressed by one of his teammates. That was Charlie Scott, who had tied Kentucky's Dan Issel for Rookie of the Year honors the past season. Scott was another New York-bred ballplayer who had matured in the ghetto playgrounds and developed the hard-nosed go-to-the-basket game that was so stimulating to watch. The six-six guard loved to shoot and had finished fifth in the ABA scoring race as a freshman, ripping the nets for an average of 27.1 points a game. Julius was looking forward to their becoming the team's dynamic duo, combining to give the Squires the kind of firepower that would tally at least half the team's scoring. Scott would pour them in from the outside, while Julius would dunk and drive and put in rebounds.

It may have sounded like a rookie's pipe dream, but that was exactly the way it went from the opening game of the season. Going against the Carolina Cougars to begin their 1971–72 schedule, Virginia registered a 118–114 victory. Scott headed the pointmakers with 36, while Julius' first pro contribution was 21 points and a solid rebounding job.

The one-two punch from Virginia practically duplicated their showing in the Squires' second game, when Scott weighed in with 37 points and Julius notched 20. But the rest of the team couldn't match the pace they set, and the Squires suffered their first defeat of the year, 94–93, to Memphis.

With Scott and Julius running wild, with Scott gunning at the hoop every chance he got, and with Julius scoring and rebounding up front, Bianchi saw that he had the makings of a squad that could run all season long. The roster had some veterans, but its primary assets were youth, vigor, and the sort of racehorse vitality that could outleg most opponents into exhaustion. A team could win plenty of games that way, especially against opposition that ran out of steam by the fourth quarter. Furthermore, it was the nonstop style of basketball that kept a crowd in a fever from start to finish.

However, there were critics of this wide-open game of all shooting and no defense. After Virginia had lost to the lowly Pittsburgh Condors, 149–136, one sportswriter noted:

Charlie Scott's point totals look great on paper, but have you ever checked his statistics? He misses more than he makes. Give him the ball and he can be counted on to heave the ball at the basket just about every time, rather than let someone else try his luck. The records show he's averaging five assists a game but, for the life of me, I can't see where they got those figures.

Scott's hot-shot gunnery is typical of the ABA's major failing. Too many players are point-happy and the front offices think that's what the fans want to see—a shootout, a pop-pop-pop, up-the-floor-down-the-floor exhibition of who can score more or faster than the other guys. That's not the way basketball should be played in the pros, and they should take some lessons from the older league. In the NBA, defense is as much a part of the game as offense. Even the fast-break teams, like the Boston Celtics, pay strict attention to defense when they don't have possession. That's known as strategy, something the fans understand and consider when they watch two teams in action.

Pro-class basketball *is* on display regularly—in the NBA. That's where Bill Russell made defense a weapon, and where Kareem Abdul-Jabbar is intimidating whole teams with his stop-'em or scare-'em style That's where an entire team, the New York Knickerbockers, become a unit that switches and double-teams every time the other side invades their turf. It's called complete basketball, and that's something the ABA has to stage in its arenas if it's going to grow up and become more than the younger brother of the NBA.

Defenders of the ABA faith in high-scoring games disagreed. They argued that the heart of the game was making points, that the fans loved action and spectacular shows and were bored by slow, thoughtful basketball. Johnny Kerr was one of the spokesmen for the pulse-pounding offensive game, and he predictably praised both Scott and Erving. While he acknowledged that Julius was more of a team man and played far more defense than Scott, he emphasized the Doctor's superb offensive talents. "You can use all the adjectives you want to describe some of Julius Erving's moves," Kerr said. "I promise you, once this kid makes his first swing around the league, and people see what he can do, he's going to draw crowds the rest of the year."

Scott was also spreading the word about Dr. J.

"Now I've got someone to run with," he said. "And he rebounds well. Don't forget, rebounding was one of our weak points last year. Kentucky has improved by getting Artis Gilmore, who's doing a great job at center, but we're not giving up hope that we can beat them."

As the season progressed, Virginia and Kentucky maintained their head-to-head battle for first place in the Eastern Division. With seven-foot two-inch rookie center Artis Gilmore shot-blocking and rebounding at 20 caroms a contest, to complement Dan Issel's average of 30 points a game, the Colonels were tough. Virginia's determined challenge to Kentucky's performances was focused on the double-barreled threat of Scott and Erving. Scott's 37-point average was leading the league, while Julius was shooting at a 23-points-a-game clip and taking away rebounds at close to 17 a game.

By the end of November Kentucky's coach, Joe Mullaney, evaluated the Virginia squad: "Virginia doesn't look so deep, personnel-wise," he said. "But they play the best defense against us. They impress me with the way they play defense. They bother the heck out of us. We have to work harder against them than anyone else. Yet what puzzles me is that I see them losing to lesser clubs, and I have to wonder if they just do something against us that makes them look so super."

Mullaney's question wasn't hard to answer. Although Scott was concentrating on maintaining his top-of-the-list scoring pace, the rest of the Virginia lineup was turning in more defense than the ABA was accustomed to seeing. Dr. J was a vital factor in hampering the offensive strategies of Kentucky and other scoring machines in the league. Hounding his own man on defense, Julius also would go to the aid of teammates by dropping off his man and pestering the opposition's hot-shooting centers, forwards, or guards whenever he could. And his brilliant leaping and instinctive timing threatened to make endangered species of unwary rival shooters who were unaccustomed to such shot-blocking maneuvers. On top of that, his quick hands continually deflected passes and picked up an occasional steal. This steady diet of frustration helped the Squires upset teams like Kentucky, teams used to speeding upcourt and dashing off their plays without more than token resistance.

Erving's total effort charged up his teammates, and they tried their utmost to copy his make-them-earn-it defense. Forward Neil Johnson and center Jim Eakins doubled their exertions to keep pace with the example-setting rookie, and freshman Willie Sojourner gained experience and inspiration just by being on the floor with the scintillating Dr. J. This display of hustle and grit encouraged veterans like guard Doug Moe and forward Ray Scott to reach deeper for skills and physical reserves they hadn't used for a while.

Almost single-handedly, Dr. J was lifting the team onto a higher plane. His urge to win was infectious, and the entire squad was developing an unexpected confidence, steadily growing convinced of its potential to capture the division title and then go all the way to the championship.

Virginia was riding high in first place on November 12, when Julius invaded New York for his first time as a pro. The Squires were in town to play the Nets, who were in third place, just a couple of games behind Virginia. To match Scott and Erving, the Nets had a torrid-shooting duet in forward Rick Barry and guard Bill Melchionni.

Long Island fans were anxiously anticipating this clash of high-flying teams and their hot-handed scorers. But their loyalties were divided. While they were pulling for their hometown Nets to edge up in the standings, they were equally hopeful that their own Dr. J would produce a few of his dazzling eye-popping forays to the basket. These were the moves that made grown men gasp and young boys slap hands and chortle, "That's the Doctor, operating again. He's something else!"

That afternoon, several hours before game time, Julius went home to visit his mother. Then he attended a get-together with some friends. It was a high point in his life, and just before the game he told a reporter, "I went over to the old elementary school, Theodore Roosevelt, to see some people. We talked about the old times and about what I was doing now. I thought about the game often during the day. It was special, and I wanted a good game."

It wasn't just a good game; it was a great one. Rick Barry responded to the challenge and scored 38 points, and Bill Melchionni added 27. As usual, Charlie Scott showed everybody the way with 42, although his defensive play wasn't overwhelming. As for Julius, he got 29 points, racked up 17 rebounds, and kept his faithful followers in full cry with stunning acrobatics. Their response delighted him, but what was most soul-satisfying was Virginia's 127–123 overtime victory.

At this point, nothing was going to worry the hero who had returned home in triumph. But it wasn't long afterward that his success caused the kind of problems that every hero encounters. It was the price he had to pay for being a superstar, and he didn't take pleasure in it.

6

First-Year Problems

When it came time for voting to determine the players who would take part in the ABA's 1972 All-Star game, the name of Julius Erving was as well known as any in the league. Virginia was still running neck and neck with Kentucky for the lead in their division, and even though Charlie Scott was well ahead of all competition with better than 35 points, it was Dr. J who was being credited as the number one reason for the Squires' unexpected success.

Typical of the raves coming Julius' way was the statement made by Alex Hannum, coach of the Denver Rockets. "Erving's the best thing that has happened to our league," Hannum said. "He turns the whole town on. They can't wait for him to come back."

Hannum was describing the reaction of Denver fans, a reaction that was being repeated in every city around the ABA circuit. Hannum emphasized that it wasn't just Dr. J's scoring and rebounding that was magnetizing fans. It was, above everything else, his flamboyant style. The response of fans around the league was strongest in Virginia, where

Charlie Scott had been the crowd pleaser until Julius leaped onto the scene. Almost immediately, it was Julius, not Scott, who got the loudest ovation from the stands when the lineup was being introduced. It was Julius, not Scott, who caught the writers' fancy and got the most coverage on the sports pages. It was reaching the point where rumors were starting to spread that Scott was so unhappy that he wanted to be traded or he would jump to the NBA.

The situation grew worse as the season moved along. In an interview with one reporter, Coach Bianchi assessed the Erving-Scott dilemma as it had developed from the beginning of the season. "We had a definite problem there," the Virginia coach recalled. "The fans naturally gravitated from Charlie to Julie. Julie was thrilling on the court and so mature off it. Charlie was just a child.

"To balance Julie's dominance, Charlie wanted to win the league scoring title. He knew it. Julie knew it. I knew it. Julie was mature enough to accept it and fit his own game to that fact.

"Charlie would shoot and shoot. One night he scored forty-nine points, and afterward I told him he played a terrible game."

Bianchi attempted to teach Scott that no player can win games all by himself. As important as scoring is, the team will fail unless it functions as a five-man unit for four quarters of every game. Bianchi also tried to make Scott see that, without the help of his teammates, he could lose his chance to win the scoring title. They could, if they wanted to, choose to not pass him the ball to make all those shots possible. For example, what if Julius decided to go for the basket himself instead of feeding the ball to other players?

But Scott didn't seem to see anything but his loss of importance, and he didn't seem to hear anything but the crescendo of cheers that greeted Julius every time the Squires took the floor.

For all the team's success, it was becoming a season of discontent for the Squires. It was the sort of thing that can become contagious. Scott was helping spread it with his off-court complaints and on-court play-for-Charlie campaign, and the newspapers were doing their share by publicizing it on the sports pages.

The contagion of dissatisfaction finally got to the even-tempered Dr. J. Among the league's finest rebounders and scorers, the crowd-drawing young Squire took a closer look at how other ABA rookies were doing, both as players and salary earners. What he saw was that only Kentucky center Artis Gilmore was making as many waves as he—and that Gilmore was earning *four* times as much money as he was being paid. Other high-priced first-year players were Johnny Neumann, who was getting $2,000,000 from Memphis, and Jim McDaniels, who had signed a $2,900,000 contract with Carolina. Julius knew he was worth a great deal more than the $500,000 he had agreed to. Not only did that bother him in terms of dollars, but it also hurt his pride.

So Julius sat down with his representative, Bob Woolf, and asked the lawyer to renegotiate his contract. When Woolf told Julius that he didn't think it was the right thing to do, Julius turned to another agent for help. He was Irwin Weiner, who represented a number of big-name athletes, including Walt Frazier, the high-salaried guard of the New York Knickerbockers.

Weiner carried Julius' request to Earl Foreman. But the Squires' owner had no intention of parting with any more money. Not only wouldn't he give Julius a raise, he wouldn't even give him the $50,000 he had agreed to pay Julius over a period of years (in order to save him tax payments), but to which Julius was entitled any time he asked for it.

Weiner felt justified in trying to make a deal for Dr. J with other teams, since Foreman had gone back on his promise regarding the $50,000. One team that seemed a good bet was the NBA's Atlanta Hawks. That team's owner, Bill Putnam, had been burned twice by the ABA, once when the younger league had snatched away his star center, Zelmo Beaty, and again when his excellent forward Joe Caldwell jumped to an ABA team.

Weiner and Putnam came to terms, a five-year contract that would reward Julius with far more money then he was getting from Virginia, as well as other benefits, including a new car and a paid-for apartment in Atlanta.

It was another skirmish in the ever-expanding NBA-ABA war, and while it was being called "dirty" and "sneaky" by some owners and sportswriters, it was becoming so commonplace that no one was particularly surprised by this latest chapter involving Julius.

Bill Putnam also had a better argument than some other owners who had gained players by this method of dealing. He pointed out that Julius' UMass class would be graduating in a few months, and that was the time when Dr. J would truly be eligible for the NBA college draft. Of course, Putnam was choosing to ignore the fact that Julius was not the property of Atlanta and couldn't even be considered a potential Hawk unless the Doctor were named by the Hawks in the draft that would take place in April—four months away.

Putnam also chose to disregard the NBA rule that required all league owners to honor ABA contracts. That rule was established to keep the player-snatching war from becoming worse than it already was.

When Putnam was asked why he was acting in defiance of the rule, he said, "I view the Erving situation as being identical to the Spencer Haywood situation." The NBA's SuperSonics had signed Haywood, even though he was ABA property, and had gotten away with it. Thus, Putnam argued, "Haywood had signed a contract before his class graduated, and so he was eligible for our draft. He was already a pro, in the ABA. What's the difference between Haywood's case and Erving's?"

There may have been no difference from Putnam's point of view, but he neglected to do one very important thing—and it made an already-muddled situation even more muddled. When the NBA draft took place on April 10, 1972, the Milwaukee Bucks—not the Atlanta Hawks—drafted Julius Erving on the first round. This would prove of great significance in the near future.

Although this behind-closed-doors wheeling and dealing was supposed to be done with only the knowledge of Julius, Weiner, and the Hawks' front office, word was beginning to leak out. One of the people who got wind of it was Charlie Scott. But unfortunately for him, it didn't reach him until after he had made his own deal to escape the ABA for the greener fields of the NBA. Once he had definitely wrapped up the ABA scoring title, Scott announced that he was deserting the Squires and the ABA for the NBA's Phoenix Suns.

This confusing business had begun in January and was to continue almost to the end of the season, mid-April, 1972. But Julius had determined that whatever the final results would be, he was not going to let the wheeling and dealing interfere with his major interest: playing basketball. He'd let his agent worry about the contract situation while he concentrated on his game-by-game performances. That was the kind of "warfare" he understood and could handle best of all.

By the end of January Julius had upped his scoring average beyond the 26-points-a-game level, and his 15.7-rebounds-a-game average had elevated him into third position in the carom race. However, the rest of the Squires, with the exception of basket-hungry Charlie Scott, had not matched Julius' caliber of play, and the team had slipped to 9½ games behind the Kentucky Colonels in the struggle for first place.

Then the league took time out for the All-Star game.

Julius was chosen for the Eastern Division squad —but not among the starting five. However, he more than made up for that oversight once he entered the game, which was played at Kentucky's Freedom Hall in Lexington.

By the time the fireworks were over and the screams of the crowd were echoes, the East squad was relaxing and delightedly reviewing the highlights of their 142–115 annihilation of the Western Division All-Stars. One of the most satisfied winners was Dr. J. In twenty-five minutes of playing time, Julius had pumped in 20 points, grabbed 3 rebounds, and fed off for 3 baskets. It was the opinion of many that the game's turning point came when the Doctor and fellow rookies Jim McDaniels and Artis Gilmore were on the court together. One of the players voicing that feeling was the Nets' guard, Bill Melchionni, who said, "We really moved the ball. It's fantastic, the improvement in this game from the last two I was in. There were three rookies out there—McDaniels, Erving, and Gilmore—when we broke it up, and they were in there against the likes of Mel Daniels and Zelmo Beaty, when we went from ten points ahead to twenty."

Weighing in with his personal observations of the contest was Jim O'Brien, a New York sportswriter covering the game for *The Sporting News*. Writing in that publication, O'Brien said:

One of the precocious kids who turned the game, which was certainly the best in the young league's history, into a rout was Julius (Dr. J.) Erving. . . .

It was still a contest until Dr J., with his fat bag of tricks, began to operate early in the third quarter. Erving, who under normal circumstances would be a senior at the University of Massachusetts, scored eight of the East's 18 points in a scoring tear that broke a 67–67 tie and carried the victors to a six-point edge at 85–79.

Several of Erving's forays to the basket were

of the sensational variety. He was certainly the most spectacular performer in this nationally televised game. On the spectacular stuff by Erving, John Kerr was seen shaking his head from where he sat under the basket.

"After all the games I've seen him play this year," commented Kerr afterward, "he still brings me out of my seat. I've played over a thousand games in this sport myself and he still shakes me up. He's electrifying, that's for sure."

One indicator of the difference between Julius and fellow All-Star Charlie Scott showed up in the game's statistics. While the shot-happy guard had connected on 9 out of 21 shots from the floor—a poor shooting percentage—Julius had sunk 9 out of 15, an admirable 60 percent. And while Julius' work had earned him a number of nominations for the Most Valuable Player Award (which went to Dan Issel), Scott's name was barely mentioned. It was another thorn in Scott's side, another reason for him to want to pull up stakes and escape Erving territory for the money and glory awaiting him in the NBA.

Still, there was plenty of basketball to be played in the second half of the season. Scott had to withstand the challenges of Issel and Rick Barry, who were running about 4 points behind his torrid list-topping pace of 35 points a game. And Julius had to maintain his own high standards of scoring, rebounding, and team leadership, no matter where he would be playing the next season.

But something vital had gone out of the Virginia Squires. Perhaps it was because the team's rookies were feeling the pressure of a tight race and couldn't handle it as well as such veterans as Kentucky's. Perhaps the team's confidence was being sapped by the Scott-Erving conflict and the rumors that both their superstars would be playing elsewhere next year. Or perhaps it was because opponents were keying their defenses more and more on Dr. J, aware that he was the cornerstone of the Squires' success.

Whatever the reason, the Squires couldn't keep step with the Kentucky Colonels, who surged ahead and eventually turned the Eastern Division race into a rout. When the season finally wound down, the Colonels had outdistanced runner-up Virginia by 23 games. It was a dispirited Squires' squad at the end of the season, and there was little hope that they would do much in the upcoming championship play-offs.

7

The Game Goes On

If the Squires had faded when the going got tough, it was no fault of the fabulous Dr. J. Everyone knew what his leadership and unselfish play had meant to the team throughout the 84-game season. Everyone knew that he had been the core of the enthusiastic club that had been contenders for the first half of the season and the glue that had tried to hold them together over the second half. And of course, he was credited with being the league's incomparable drawing card, *the* player who drew fans in droves to arenas that had previously been suffering low-attendance blues.

Julius had done well for the Squires, the ABA, and himself. The superrookie came in sixth in the 1971–72 scoring race. His 27.26-points-a-game average was well behind run-and-gun Charie Scott's record-setting 34.58 mark, but it was nothing to be ashamed of, particularly for a rookie on a poorly balanced team. The Doctor also made his presence felt in the battles under the boards, winding up third in rebounding with an average of 15.7 a game, as compared with the league-leading carom count of 17.8 a game posted by Artis Gilmore.

Then, as if to prove that he could do it if he wanted to, Julius used the postseason play-offs to catapult himself to the head of the class in both scoring and rebounding. In the eleven games Virginia played, in which the Squires bounced back from their gloom to trounce the Floridians in four straight games before bowing to the Nets in six contests, Julius really opened up.

Free now of Charlie Scott's keep-the-ball-and-shoot presence (Scott had been suspended after his NBA jump was revealed), the Doctor averaged 33.27 points a game. That was the top scoring mark in the play-offs, as was Julius' 20.36 average in rebounding.

To round off a most impressive pro debut, the league honored Julius by naming him to the ABA All-League second team and awarding him one of the two forward spots on the All-Rookie team. In the voting for Rookie of the Year, the Doctor was edged out by Kentucky's Artis Gilmore.

While all the play-offs' court action was taking place, the interleague war was heating up on the sidelines. Between games Virginia Coach Al Bianchi learned of Julius' being drafted by the Milwaukee Bucks and also that his prize rookie was seriously thinking of jumping to the Atlanta Hawks.

Bianchi didn't believe Julius would jump or didn't

want to believe it. When the coach was asked what he thought of the rumors, he said, "They're not true. I asked Julie about it this morning, I said, 'Hey, Julie, what's going on here? Every day I read that you're signing with this club or that club. Have you signed with any NBA team?' He said he hadn't, and I have to believe him." But Bianchi was aware that something was cooking because the rumor mill continued to grind out stories that Julius was on his way elsewhere.

As for Charlie Scott's move to the Phoenix Suns, Bianchi didn't seem to be overly upset. "We're glad," he said, "that Charlie's finally with a team where he has someone to pass the ball off to."

Bianchi's sarcastic dig at Scott was accompanied by a smile, but he found it considerably harder to smile at the ominous prospect of losing his ace scorer-rebounder. He wanted to believe what Julius had told him and to feel assured that the Doctor would be operating in Virginia the next season. Yet he had been around long enough to be wary of any possibility.

And so Bianchi's last words on the subject, that "Julie is a different kind of kid from Scott," were hardly out of his mouth when the storm broke. Julius had, indeed, chosen to wear a Hawk uniform the next season.

It appeared certain that Julius was NBA-bound, but he was a member of the ABA lineup on May 25,

1972, when the ABA All-Stars faced the NBA All-Stars in a game described as featuring "the finest collection of basketball talent ever assembled on one floor." Wilt Chamberlain, Oscar Robertson, John Havlicek, and Nate Archibald were among the NBA's superstars, while Artis Gilmore, Rick Barry, Dan Issel, and Dr. J were the big guns of their ABA opposition.

The game was a beauty, with the NBA eking out a 106–104 victory. And Julius, chipping in with 13 points and a display of his incomparable moves, was a thing of beauty all by himself. Daring the mighty Chamberlain and Bob Lanier, Dr. J spun and soared to the basket with his patented high-wire act in full bloom. It was, in one observer's words, "a sight for bored eyes."

One particular Erving maneuver tickled Bob Love and Archie Clark of the NBA, who were sitting on the bench. After gaping at Julius lift off like a rocket and complete his flight with a backboard-shivering slam, Love chuckled and nudged Clark in the ribs. "Now, wasn't that something?" Love said. "The man took off at the free throw line."

"What are you going to do?" Clark answered. "You can't help but appreciate all that talent. It's just a good feeling to see someone express himself like that. That's the beauty of All-Star games."

It was the sort of court miracle that made coaches like Al Bianchi wish the owners would settle down and just let the players do the one thing they did naturally and happily: play the game on the floor, not the one that took place over bargaining tables.

Julius put the summer of '72 to good use, preparing himself for the coming season. If his agent's actions were successful, Dr. J would be performing his trapeze act for the NBA's Hawks. If they weren't, he would be back with the Squires. Julius wasn't sure where he'd be playing, but he was sure he'd be playing somewhere, so he practiced. And practice for him had to have a purpose as well as be fun, which compelled him to concentrate on what he considered his greatest weakness, outside shooting.

With the beginning of the Hawks' preseason training camp, in September, Julius reported to Atlanta Coach Cotton Fitzsimmons. The coach immediately sent him out to work with Pete Maravich, the guard of a million moves, many of which were unpredictable. Pete was to guards what Julius was to forwards —a many-splendored creator of the astonishing play —except that Pete's teammates often didn't know what he had in mind while Julius' teammates almost always knew what was coming.

Between them, Pistol Pete and Dr. J were capable of creating a circus of sparkling showmanship. But Fitzsimmons cautioned them, if they didn't discipline themselves to cooperate, Atlanta would end up with the most entertaining team *and* the worst record in the history of the NBA. The last thing the

Hawks wanted was a repeat of the Erving-Scott situation in Virginia.

As it turned out, Fitzsimmons' fears were erased by the legal courts. While Julius and Pete were playing gorgeous basketball in a pair of Hawk exhibition games, executing the give-and-go and fast break to perfection, a judge was concluding that the Doctor had to honor his contract with the Squires.

Julius' agent appealed the verdict, but while Julius was awaiting the outcome of the appeal, he was a player without a team. All through September and much of October he worked out with friends, staying in shape, determined to be ready when the call came for him to join either the Hawks or the Squires.

The call came at last, near the end of October, and it was from Virginia. The Squires, who had already played and lost four regular-season games, were jubilant at the prospect of the return of Dr. J. Equally up were the fans, even though it had been feared that they might reject Julius for deserting them for the NBA. But it became quickly clear that Dr. J's popularity and gate appeal were as strong as ever.

Al Bianchi explained why Julius received such a warm welcome on his return. "He is the kind of guy who never closes doors behind him," the Virginia coach said. "Charlie Scott could never have returned and been accepted. But no matter where Julius might go, they would always love him here."

As for his own feelings, Bianchi said, "There was never any question that I wanted Julius back or how well he would play once he got here. His play-off totals for us show that he actually played better after he had signed with the Hawks. That's the kind of guy he is."

The kind of player he was also was in evidence from his first night back in action. Netting 26 points and grabbing 11 rebounds in thirty minutes of play against the New York Nets, Julius carried Virginia to its first victory of the young season, 130–120.

After the game he shared the joy of his teammates in the locker room, then said, "All I want to prove is that I can be the best forward in basketball. I can prove that in either league."

When he was asked if the lack of practice with the team had affected his game, Julius said, "It affected me mostly on defense and rebounding, where hustle counts the most. I still have all the moves, though, and it won't take me long to get back into top shape."

If the first game was, in Julius' estimation, below par, the league had a great deal to look forward to. As Julius geared his body and mind into the groove, the Squires benefited from his "below par" efforts. In their second game with Julius in the lineup, the Virginias beat Carolina, 119–110, and the Doctor contributed 23 points. Then they followed up with two more wins, as he found the range for 35 and 22 points.

Now the Erving-led squad had evened its record at 4 wins and 4 losses, and Virginia's bubbly guard, Roland "Fatty" Taylor, went around bragging about "my man, the Doctor." After one victory, over the Nets, Taylor said, "It's great to have him back. I had missed him on the fast break. The things he can do with a basketball should be against the law.

"In the second period, I saw him coming out of the right corner and across the lane, where he likes to get the ball. I was facing him and fed him the pass. He went up with the ball in his right hand, but Billy Paultz was all over him. So he simply switched it to his left hand and got a three-point play out of it that left the fans in the aisles."

While Taylor was describing that moment, in the New York locker room, losing Coach Lou Carnesecca was saying, "Erving is the most exciting pro ever. Thank God that Bianchi didn't start him. He did enough damage to us in the time he *was* in. He creates. It just flows out of him. He has great imagination on the court. You can talk about this guy the way you'd talk about a poet. He *is* a poet, an artist, when he's on the court."

The basketball poetry of Dr. J continued as the season advanced. But not even his artistry could fashion victory for a Squires' team that had more desire than ability. By the time the 1973 All-Star break came, Virginia was 11 games out of first place and showing no signs of getting any better.

Julius, however, remained a champion in attitude and performance. As a member of the Eastern Division All-Star squad, he topped their scoring with 22 points in thirty minutes. But his effort, as it was too often with Virginia, was wasted as the Western All-Stars took the game, 123–111.

Then, two days later, on February 8, a charged-up Julius squared off against the Nets for a game on the Squires' home court. It was as if he were still facing the best in the West as he powered through, over, or around the New York defenders in a basket barrage that totaled 56 points with time remaining on the clock. A time-out was called, and the Squires collected around their coach. Then the team trainer asked Bianchi, "Are you going to let him go for the record?"

"What record?" Bianchi answered.

"The league scoring record."

"What is it?" Bianchi said.

"It's sixty-seven points."

Bianchi pointed at the clock, which showed just one minute and fourteen seconds remaining in the game. "He'd have to get eleven points in that time. Who do you think he is, Superman?"

The trainer didn't answer, but his expression seemed to be saying, "Yes, on a basketball court."

The game was completed, a 123–108 win for the Squires, and a 58-point effort by Dr. J, including 22 straight shots from the free throw line. And the superscorer told reporters, "I don't know if it was my best game or not, but I know I felt good shooting. I came back after the All-Star game and got plenty of rest. My jump shot is back with me now, and it has opened up my inside game."

Bianchi thought Julius had been even more impressive against the Floridians in one of the 1972 play-off games. "Julius scored fifty-three points and took down twenty-two rebounds in that one," Bianchi recalled. "Points, rebounds, assists . . . Julius just does what we need him to do.

"There's no question that his outside shot has improved this season," the coach went on. "As far as his defense is concerned, it depends on the game and the situation. At times, it's real good. And at times, it's not so good. We depend on him so much offensively it's not fair to be finding fault with his defensive play."

As the season wound down, with the Squires solidly mired in third place in their division, Julius injured his back slightly. Since the team was going nowhere anyway, it was decided that Julius should sit out a few games rather than risk further injury. Bianchi left the team to scout the Kentucky Colonels, whom the Squires would be playing in the first round of the play-offs. In his place as substitute coach for the final game of the regular season was none other than second-year pro Julius Erving.

With Dr. J. coolly directing the team from the sidelines, the Squires downed the New York Nets, 121–106. Even off the court he was the team leader providing inspiration, and his 1–0 coaching record prompted John Kerr to say, "It just goes to prove that they still can't win without Julie. His pride and desire just reach everybody."

That final victory enabled the Squires to end the season with a .500 percentage, behind Carolina and Kentucky. But not even Julius' 29.6-a-game scoring could save them from early elimination by Kentucky, four games to one, in the postseason playoffs.

Throughout the Squires' up-and-down season of 42 wins and 42 losses, Julius refused to be bogged down by the inability of his teammates. And it was clear that it was his one-man battle against crushing odds that kept Virginia from sinking into the cellar of the Eastern Division. As a result, he was named to the ABA All-Star team for the second straight year, as one of the two top forwards. He won that distinction by capturing his first league scoring crown, averaging almost 32 points a game and finishing well ahead of runner-up George McGinnis; by wowing rooters and players alike with his magnificent offense and constantly improving defense, not the least of which was a steady run of blocked shots; by rebounding at the rate of 12.2 a game, which was sixth best in the league and just a fraction below the men who finished in the three places above him; and by coming in third in steals, plucking the ball away from rivals 181 times. The steals were particularly impressive since guards, not forwards, are the players who most often play the role of ball thief.

How, basketball buffs wondered, was Julius able to perform so superbly on a team so weak? How was he able to do it night after night when he wasn't sure where he would be playing the next season? That was a real problem, one that had to be on his mind day and night, on the court and off. Talk was that the entire Virginia franchise was in financial trouble and that Julius might be sold by owner Earl Foreman, who needed money to stay in busines.

Dr. J's teammate, Fatty Taylor, provided part of the answer. "I was telling my friends in Washington, D.C., about Julius," Taylor said, "about how great he is. Some of them just didn't believe one man could be all that great. So I asked Julius if he'd come with me to Washington and play in a benefit game."

Julius could have said no, since he was set to play in the ABA-NBA All-Star game in New York the night before the Washington game. "Because of that," Taylor went on, "my friends didn't think he'd accept. But there was a lot they didn't know about him. He showed up, all right. All he did was score fifty points, grab twenty-some rebounds, and make ten moves I didn't see all season. He was the talk of the town for two weeks. Some of my friends came up to me and said, 'I still can't believe what I saw.'

"What they didn't know, when they were telling me that he wouldn't come, was that he'd go anywhere to play basketball. That's why I knew he'd show. He wants everyone to know he's the best."

Dunking, destroying defenders with his swoop-high-and-by flights for drop-in two-pointers, whirling and whamming home reverse lay-ups, keeping the defense honest by hitting the hoop on one-handers from fifteen and twenty feet out, Dr. J was on the way to building a reputation as the "most" forward the game had ever seen.

Testimony to his matchless play came from players in the ABA and NBA and from officials with other teams. Doug Moe, who had played in the Virginia backcourt, gave his views on the development of Dr. J. "The first time I ever saw him warm up, I thought, 'Oh, no, here we go again. He's just another showboat.' But I couldn't have been more wrong. Julius was the most mature rookie I'd ever seen. When he does something out of the ordinary, he's really only using his body to best advantage.

"He comes at you with those long, open strides, and you have a tendency to keep backing away from him because you think he's not really into his move yet. If you keep backing, if you fail to go up and challenge him, he'll simply glide right by you.'

Then there was the praise from Atlanta Hawk

forward Jim Washington, whose job was in danger when it looked as though Julius would be playing NBA ball. "Erving utilizes most of his moves on fast breaks or semifast breaks," Washington said, "so they're not out of context. It's not like we set up half court, give him the ball, and he took off on his own. He acts in keeping with the flow of the team."

And Carolina Cougar General Manager Carl Scheer joined the camp of Erving praisers by saying, "Julius will keep people in the arena until the last minute because they're afraid if they leave, he might do something nobody's ever seen before or ever will again. He looks like a hot dog, but everything he does has a purpose if you analyze it."

One mind-blowing move came in a game against San Diego. It was recounted by a sports reporter, who wrote:

"Erving leaped far out from the board with a defensive rebound and, as opponents have begun to do this season to prevent him from taking off on the fast break, one of the Conquistadors jumped in front of him as he went back up into the air to pass. The right-handed lob he planned to throw would have been deflected, so Erving, suddenly airborne, turned 360 degrees (a complete circle), changed hands, and flipped a high left-handed pass off his hip before he landed. The ball sailed over the retreating defense and dropped into the hands of teammate Bernie Williams, who took it at full speed and scored a layup.

That miracle of physical and mental instinct also stunned San Diego's assistant coach, Stan Albeck. "Man," he gasped, "I thought I'd seen everything. But that three-hundred-sixty-degree job. . . . Nobody's ever done anything like that. It was unbelievable."

To see is to believe, and when it came to Dr. J with a ball in his hand, anything was believable.

But the last word on the subject of Julius Erving came from the Doctor himself. Speaking about his thunderclap-dramatic crowd-captivating plays, he pointed out the sense and logic of such moves. For example, on the subject of his sky's-the-limit dunks, he said, "The no-dunking rule came into being during my senior year in high school, so I hadn't been allowed to slam in competition for four years. When I first started playing in the pros, I couldn't get enough of it. Now, if I can score on a simple lay-up, I usually will, except if I think our team needs a big dunk. It's all psychological then. If we're down a few points and I'm fast-breaking, I'll sometimes decide that the time has come to get freaky. It gets the crowd up, and our team, and me. Because of the excitement, we'll often start to defend better, to make good plays, and to pull ahead. But overall, I'd have to say that, as I get older, my game gets more conservative."

He was an "ancient" twenty-two and already talking like an elder statesman of the game, as if he were a veteran reminiscing about a long, illustrious career. In fact, he was just a two-year professional who had to suspect, deep down, that his most superslick, non-conservative games were still to come.

8

Number One in the ABA

Virginia fans came to see the Julius Erving Magic Show, but not even Dr. J could keep the faithful followers flowing through the turnstiles when the Squires revealed they were a mediocre team going downhill in the competition for the division flag. Poor attendance meant poor income, and money is the lifeblood of any business, especially professional basketball. By the end of the 1972–73 season, owner Earl Foreman's books were showing a deficit of $700,000.

His solution was the same as it has been when the profit picture had looked bleak and Rick Barry couldn't continue to bring in the fans. He had sold Barry then, and he decided to sell his most valuable player now. That meant Julius Erving was on the market.

Among the most interested shoppers was Ray Boe, owner of the New York Nets. Boe had kept his eyes open for a star to draw fans into his Long Island arena, ever since the much-traveled Rick

Barry had returned to the NBA. Boe gave Foreman $1,000,000 and forward George Carter and received the services of Julius Erving in exchange.

Boe then held a press conference, introducing Dr. J as the priceless bargain who had "come home" to play for the people he had grown up with.

Julius was glad to be back, most of all because he could be close to his mother. But he also kept in mind that the Nets' fans would be counting on him to bring them an ABA title *and* perform wondrous deeds in every game.

After reminding Julius of these expectations, a reporter asked him "Doesn't all this put a great deal of pressure on you?"

Julius considered the question carefully, then answered, "I put the most pressure on myself because of my ambitions to be the best professional basketball player ever. . . . What happens around me can't put any more pressure on me than that."

Following the press conference, Julius went to visit a place he knew well, one he had visited every year since he had gone away to the University of Massachusetts—Roosevelt Park. It hadn't changed. Boys still came there to tangle in the one-on-one shoot-outs that could win fame for the really "tough" competitors. There were new neighborhood stars with their eyes on the skies and dreams in their hearts. And their biggest dream was one day to be as great as Dr. J, whose name was on a sign at Roosevelt Park, with the inscription, "This is where Julius Erving learned to play basketball."

And there, on the asphalt court where the young Julius Erving had taken the first steps to becoming the man he was now, Dr. J was greeted by the players who knew him then and the ones who had grown up in the years between.

One of the "old-timers," James Maxwell, grinned at the sight of the returning hero. "Julius is the most creative man I've seen out there," Maxwell told a group of youngsters. "He's the best playground player . . . the best player anywhere."

Another hometown admirer of Julius, Ricky Whitfield, added, "When he comes to the park, he talks with everybody. He's a pro, he doesn't have to do that, but he does. That's why I idolize him so much, he's so nice."

The newest Net was an idol to thousands, yet in his own opinion he was "just another man who works for a living. I like the simple things, I really do. My life-style has changed considerably, but I still want to identify with my roots. There are certain things you can't buy in life, there are things I have that people can't buy, and I don't want to give them up. Friendships, memories of people who have affected my growth and development."

In this way he was still the soft-spoken boy who had grown and developed into a wealthy and princely man of the world. But he was also the number one player on a team that had an outstanding chance to be kings of the ABA.

The New Yorkers opened the season on a sour note, however, losing 118–99 to the Indiana Pacers. It was far too early for first-year coach Kevin Loughery to be concerned, but he was disappointed since he had wanted to get off on the right foot. His key man, Dr. J, had pumped in 42 points, and the team had played the way he wanted them to—running on offense and pressing on defense, trying to wear down the opposition.

Playing the same way turned the trick for the Nets in their next four games, as they won behind Julius' net-rippling totals of 38, 32, 23, and 33 points. Now 4–1 in the early going, the New Yorkers were tied for first with the Kentucky Colonels.

They had zoomed out to a tremendous start, but knowledgeable critics could pick out weaknesses even while they were winning. Loughery saw them, too, but he wanted to be patient. There were rookies in the lineup, and the players had to get used to one another's styles.

Nevertheless, the Nets weren't meshing as a unit. Each man was doing his own "thing," showing little desire to sacrifice individuality for the good of the whole team. In every one of those early games the squad would start off with five players behaving like the star, seeking an opportunity to go for the basket rather than set a pick, pass off, or run a play. They would manage to keep the score close until sometime in the third or fourth quarter, and then, when they started to fall behind, they all would depend on Julius to pull out the game for them.

Guard Brian Taylor expressed the feelings of the whole team when he said, "We were all standing around, looking for Dr. J. We expected him to pick up the burden. We expected him to do it by himself. We had no closeness, no rapport."

Dr. J was coming through, but that kind of success couldn't last.

Predictably, the Nets' fortunes reversed, and they lost five games in a row. The players were beginning to gripe at one another, the rookies grew more confused and uncertain, and the crowds at Nassau Coliseum were becoming impatient with their would-be champions.

Even though the season was young, Coach Loughery decided it was time to have an open, honest talk with the team. He told them that they had made mistakes, but so had he, and that he expected everybody—including himself—to think more in terms of a total team effort. One of the points he stressed was that they couldn't make Julius the workhorse, that he had to play his role as a leader but not be the *only* one to look to when it came to clutch situations. The other teams would catch on to that and gang up on him.

Later in the year Loughery would admit, "My

original concept seemed perfectly suited to the Doctor. He plays so hard, so fast. But no one could play that way for eighty-four games. By the third week of the season I had run him into the ground. I was in the process of destroying the best player on my team, maybe in the game."

It took a great amount of practice and some critical lineup changes before the Nets could straighten out. They lost four more, bringing their losing streak to nine, before the mess was cleared up. The first good sign came in a game against the San Antonio Spurs. The team switched from its all-court press defense and began using a man-to-man style. That, along with a zone type of strategy that blocked their opponents from breaking through for easy lay-ups, forced the Spurs to shoot from the outside.

That game marked the beginning of something new, something just right, for the Nets. They defeated the Spurs by 12 points to snap their losing streak. Next came Memphis and another New York victory, 108–92. Suddenly they were rolling and practically unbeatable for the next 22 games, winning 19 and overtaking Carolina and Kentucky in the battle for top spot in the Eastern Division.

Through it all, Julius remained the kingpin of the New York club. Scoring at a rate close to 28 points a game, rebounding at an average of 11 caroms a game, blocking shots, and stealing balls, he was a demon on offense and defense. But what made the difference was that his teammates were also contributing. The Nets had discovered the secret to winning basketball, and by the All-Star break they were in first place, and Billy Paultz and Larry Kenon were picked along with Julius to play for the East's All-Star squad.

Another significant probem was solved by Loughery just before the All-Star game, when he traded good-shooting John Roche to the Kentucky Colonels for two strong, hard-hitting defense-minded players —forward Wendell Ladner and guard Mike Gale. Ladner, especially, was exactly what the Nets had to have to take the heavy load off Dr. J and Larry Kenon, who were not heavyweights and had a tough time guarding bruising forwards like Dan Issel and George McGinnis.

As Loughery planned it, while one of the super-shooters took a breather on the bench, the other would work in tandem with Ladner. On defense, Ladner would be assigned the opponent's power forward, so that Julius or Kenon wouldn't be worn out or worn down. Then, on offense, Dr. J or Dr. K would have the strength and swiftness to barrel up-court on attack.

The team was up for every game, happy to be winning and enjoying the steadily building confidence that they could go all the way. Rookie guard John Williamson, a recent college whiz and big point maker, readily adjusted to being a cog in the marvelous machine led by Dr. J. "We're all superstars," Williamson said, "but Julius is just a higher superstar than the rest of us. We don't have any jealousy. Some teams I've been on have had a couple of players who were jealous because I was the big scorer. It's not that way here. That's what I like about this team."

The other Nets voiced the same feelings, and Billy Paultz emphasized that by saying, "Earlier in the year we always wanted to get the ball to Julius—at any cost. I think it cost us some ball games. Now we go to the other guys, too. Other teams can't concentrate on Julius anymore. It's tough for them to play against an eight-man team when everyone's moving the ball. And we've learned that you're still going to get your shots, and they'll be better percentage shots, if you move it around, let everyone touch it. That's what we're doing, and the results tell the story."

The story became a fairy tale come true as the season moved on. The Nets widened the gap between themselves and the rest of the Eastern Division, and even though Julius was still leading the league in scoring and was close to the lead in other departments, he was sharing the limelight with several of his teammates. He was still the number one Net, but in a different, more meaningful way. Coach

Loughery observed, "Julius can get forty points any night he wants to, but the team wouldn't win as much. He realizes that."

If anything, it earned Julius more admiration than ever. As Carolina's coach, Larry Bown, expressed it, "I love to watch Erving play. To me, the most important thing is that he's a superstar who enjoys playing, and he puts out all the time. Kids in the stands see a superstar putting out every moment, and I think that's great for the game."

It was certainly great for the Nets, who clinched the Eastern Division title with 55 wins and 29 losses. That represented the team's best record in its seven-year existence. They definitely impressed Denver Rockets' owner, Alex Hannum, who said, "You would have to take a hard look to find a better basketball team in the country then the Nets are right now. They always have someone who can kill you, and it's usually Julius Erving."

The league's players were overwhelmingly in agreement with Hannum, as they showed when the ballots were added up for *The Sporting News* ABA Player of the Year award. It was none other than Dr. J, who swamped the field with 66 first-place votes, far ahead of runner-up Artis Gilmore's total of 17. Julius' credits were incontestable. He had finished first in the scoring race, with a 27.3 average; third place in steals (190) and blocked shots (204); sixth position in the assists category (5.1 a game); and seventh in rebounding (10.6 a game).

"He just does more and more," Coach Loughery said of his prize player. "It isn't just the points and the rebounds and the passes. It's the way he does it. I see something different every night."

And there was more to come.

9

All the Way with Dr. J!

Once Dr. J had established himself as the best forward in the ABA, basketball buffs began debating the question "Who is the best forward in all of pro basketball?" Answering that kept them busy while awaiting the start of the postseason play-offs.

Ricky Barry, the former Net who had returned to the San Francisco Warriors, had a number of boosters in the NBA. A dangerous shooter and a hustler who registered a large share of steals and assists, Barry definitely deserved nomination as the best. So comparisons were made, and one who was in a prime position to grade the two superforwards was Lou Carnesecca, who had followed Julius's career closely and had been Barry's coach with the Nets. "Julius has more flair," Carnesecca said. "Yeah, that's the way I'd put it. Julius is more creative, more imaginative. Julius is more modernistic, and Rick is more classical. Both are great artists. Both can make the clutch shots. Both can excite, both can be lethal on opponents, both have charisma, and both can make coaches look very smart."

What Carnesecca was saying was that it was almost impossible to choose between the two. But at least one player, Willie Wise of the Utah Stars, spoke out for No. 32 of the Nets. "Julius is my all-everything," Wise said. "He can do more things on the basketball court than anyone else. But when I say Rick can't do this or that, it's not a slam, because we're talking about two great ballplayers. When I was guarding Rick, he would always keep coming at me, coming at me. But Julius, it seemed, would say to himself, 'Should I go around him this time, or over him, or finesse him?' Barry kept coming at me, and Julius used to play the mind game with me. If I wanted to see the ball go in the basket, then I'd go see Rick, but if I wanted to get raised out of my seat, then I'd go see Doc."

Most people called it a tie, but there was a solid core of Erving fans who pointed out that thirty-year-old Barry was at the peak of his game, while Julius, as twenty-three, wasn't close to the bottom of his huge bag of tricks. Julius, they insisted, was just starting to develop his talents. "Give him four or five more years," said one, "and there'll be no question about who's the best."

The play for the 1974 ABA crown began for the Nets when they squared off in round one against Julius' old team, the Virginia Squires. It was like pitting a heavyweight against a middleweight boxer. The New Yorkers had finished the season a full 27 games ahead of the Squires, and they were strutting with confidence as they took the floor for the first game on their home court. The Nets took it handily and then repeated the romp in the second game, 129–110, with Julius canning 35 points, Paultz 29, and Taylor 22.

The two squads traveled to Virginia for the third game, where the overconfident Nets relaxed too long and were surprised by a 116–115 Virginia win. Dr. J and Company grew serious in a hurry, roaring back to crush the Squires, 116–88, for their third win of the series. Then they ended Virginia's season with a 108–96 win, to wrap up the series four games to one.

While New York was enjoying an easy time with the Squires, the Kentucky Colonels were having it even easier with the far more challenging Carolina Cougars, knocking them off in four straight. Kentucky seemed to be letting the Nets know they weren't going to be facing a pushover like Virginia and setting the stage for a grueling battle for the Eastern Division championship.

Round One was staged in the Nassau Coliseum. Kentucky put a formidable squad on the court, led by seven-foot two-inch Artis Gilmore, who had averaged 29.8 points and 18.5 rebounds a game against the Cougars. The Colonels also felt certain that they had a man to equal Dr. J in their own All-Star forward, Dan Issel, in addition to superior backcourt experience and fireproof led by Louie Dampier.

Billy Paultz—six eleven, 240 pounds, and very determined—took care of the Gilmore threat. In that first game Paultz pounded Gilmore, leaned on him, hounded him every step of the way, and held him to 13 points. And while Issel hit for 22 and Dampier for 21, the Colonels' attack was blunted and was no match for Dr. J's 35 points, Kenon's 20, and balanced scoring from the rest of the squad. First blood was drawn by the Nets, 119–106.

Round Two was another runaway for Loughery's team, with Gilmore and Issel being throttled by a barbed-wire Net defense while Julius led the winner's offense with 27 points in a 99–80 victory. In the third game Dr. J hooped it up for 30 points, and the Nets edged the Colonels, 89–87, on the loser's home grounds. Then the Nets wrote "The End" to any notion of a Colonel comeback by taking the series in four straight, hammering out a 103–90 win behind Julius' 27 points.

The Doctor was his steady, reliable superstar self throughout the wipeout of the Colonels. One of the major barriers that the Nets, especially Julius, had to surmount was the skyscraper defense of Gilmore. Dr. J took Gilmore in stride—the long, sweeping stride for which Julius was famous. His four-game onslaught of the Kentucky basket reached its acme in the next-to-last game. On one play the Doctor got a pass from Taylor, double-head-faked forward Jim Bradley, and angled for the basket. Between

Julius and paydirt rose the intimidating form of Gilmore, a terrifying sight to any player trying to drive for a lay-up. Well, almost any player, because Julius had eyes only for the bucket. He charged straight on, as if Gilmore didn't exist. Gilmore *was* there, one umbrellalike hand seeming to cover the hoop, but Julius rocketed on by as if Gilmore were a ghost and plunked the ball home for two points.

That play was glorious history when, with seventeen seconds left in the game and the score knotted at 87, Julius was fed an inbounds pass. Cool and confident, the playground champion taking on some hotshot, Julius simply held the ball for thirteen seconds and waited for the cock to run down almost to zero. Four seconds were left when he slid into motion, dribbled swiftly past Jim Bradley, and reached the free throw line with two seconds to go.

The gargantuan Gilmore reared up to harness Julius, who glided up. . .up. . .up, cushioned the ball in his right hand, and in full flight flicked it off his fingers at the hoop.

Swish. Two points. A Net victory.

With Kentucky bloody and beaten, only the Utah Stars stood betwen the Nets and the ABA title. Coach Kevin Loughery not only was sure his astonishing team wouldn't fold in the big series, but was sure they'd do exactly what a championship-calibre team should do.

"A lot of people figured these kids wouldn't be

able to stand the pressure of the play-offs," Loughery said, "particularly on the road against a good, experienced team like Kentucky. But after what they did down the stretch, I had hardly any doubt that they could. For more than a month they *had* to win almost every night to keep the division lead. And that's exactly what they did almost every night."

The Utah Stars knew what Julius could do, and they were banking on their own fine forward, Willie Wise, to handcuff the Doctor in the upcoming best-of-seven battle for the 1974 crown. But the most Wise could contribute in the first game at the Nassau Coliseum was 20 points on offense. On defense he was a midget against the giant that was Dr. J, who tallied 47 points and snared 10 rebounds. That point count was more than half the Nets' total in their 89–85 victory.

The second game, also in the Long Island arena, went to New York, 118–94. Julius again blitzed the Utah defense for 32 points.

While the two teams traveled to Utah, where they would resume the title fight, Adolph Rupp, the former University of Kentucky coach, was asked his opinion of the Doctor. Rupp, who had seen every great player over his fifty years in basketball, said, "Some of the best players I've ever had didn't want to take the last shot, the crucial shot. Erving's a Babe Ruth. Ruth pointed out where he was going to hit a home run, and he hit it there. Erving is the same way. Everyone in the house knows he's going to take the last shot, and he still makes it. He wants to do it because he knows he can do it. Up until now I always thought that Jerry West was the greatest baskeball player I ever saw, with Oscar Robertson right behind him, but I think right now that Julius Erving is the best."

Dr. J lived up to Rupp's expectations as the Nets captured their third straight game from the Stars, 103–100. It wasn't supposed to be so easy at the championship level, but the Nets were making it seem like a snap. Julius netted 24 points and snared 13 rebounds, while five other New Yorkers got into the act by scoring in double figures.

It appeared that Loughery's crew was going to erase the Stars in four straight. But Utah, with its shoulders against the wall and with injured center Zelmo Beaty back in the lineup, stopped the Net juggernaut with a fourth-quarter surge in Game No. 4, 97–89. But it proved to be nothing more than a slight pause in the triumphant march of the New York Nets.

Back on home turf for what turned out to be the final game, Loughery's team put it all back together for a solid conquest of Utah, 111–100. Dr. J's 16 rebounds were tops, and his 20 points were perfectly in keeping with a balanced assault that saw Kenon get 23, Paultz 21, Taylor 19, and Williamson 15.

Kings of the ABA, the Nets had gone all the way with Dr. J!

Loughery bubbled with champagne, delight, and satisfaction, and he gave nonstop credit to his team of relatively inexperienced players. "Our young squad," he told reporters during the riotous celebration in the locker room, "got more experience playing under pressure than some guys get in a lifetime. They wanted to come out on top, and no one was going to stop them."

Life couldn't have been better for Julius. He sat among his champagne-drenched teammates and laughed contentedly. "You know," he said, "this could be the kind of summer where we can't wait for the next season to start."

10

The All-Time All-Star

What could Julius and the Nets do for an encore in the 1974–75 season? Kevin Loughery's expectations were high—a repeat as Eastern Division champs, followed by a second straight ABA title. The Nets had every reason to believe they could do it again. They were a young team that had jelled into an unbeatable combination. Now they were coming back as seasoned veterans, bursting with the exhilaration of victory and expecting to be twice as good this time around.

Dr. J looked at the roster and saw an awesome scoring potential. Kenon, Williamson, Taylor, and Paultz—all of them could blister the basket, and he felt he was free to develop other aspects of his game. Defense topped his list of self-improvement. "I want to play defense differently," he said. "I want to be more physical, to lean on a man and wear him down. Defense is where games are won and lost in the pros. There are a lot of guys on our team who can score twenty. If I can play physical defense, I'll help the team. Of course, I still want the guys to depend on me when we need the big points."

Julius was thinking this way even though he had been told to be cautious about being more physical. At twenty-four, the ABA's Most Valuable Player of 1974 had knee problems. They were beginning to ache from the strain he had placed on them for so many years. One doctor said, "He's got jumper's knees. It's very common among professional players, and you can play a whole career with it. But you have to avoid the jumping and stop-and-go movements. Julius just plays too much basketball. Through the years he has played basketball seven days a week, night and day. Now he has to pace himself a bit more and not take risks that might endanger his career."

That was like telling a clock to stop running, and once the bell sounded for the 1974–75 season, Julius was off and jumping. He hit for 27, 26, and 37 points in the first three games. Even so, the Nets lost two of those contests. Wendell Ladner—the burly rough-and-ready rebounding forward—was sidelined with a knee injury, and the team's rhythm wasn't as steady as it had been at the close of the previous season. That was the signal to Julius that he, as the club's inspiration, had to keep up his scoring and rebounding while still concentrating on defense.

True to form, Julius led the way. In the next game he hit for 33, and the Nets won. In the game after that he scored 37, and the Nets won. In the next game he rang up 13 first-half points then rested his taped-up knees for the second half while his teammates coasted to victory. The following game saw him collect 20 points and 13 rebounds to power the New Yorkers to their fourth straight win. The team was back on the track, and he could ease up on his scoring and pay more attention to the other facets of the game.

With the season under full steam, it became clear that the Eastern Division would be a two-team wrestle between the Nets and their constant rivals, the Kentucky Colonels. And while the Colonels were running neck and neck with the Nets, Julius was encountering a challenge for the scoring leadership from the league's other superforward, Indiana's George McGinnis.

Dr. J and Company met all challengers in fine style, particularly when it came to facing the Colonels. A typical example was the game of January 25, with the Nets taking on the Kentuckians at Nassau Coliseum. With just three seconds to go and the score 110–110, Brian Taylor flipped in a pair of foul shots to continue the New York domination of their chief rival. Yet while Taylor's two points did it, the win wouldn't have been possible without the game-long magic of Dr. J. He scored 42 points, including 18 straight free throws, out-Gilmored Gilmore for 18 rebounds, was credited with 18 assists, and stole the ball 4 times.

Julius' scoring was all the more impressive because the Colonels were zeroing in on him as soon as he had the ball. All through the game Kentucky Coach Hubie Brown's voice could be heard booming from the bench, "Get the Doctor! Everybody help get him!"

Nothing the Colonels did could stop the Doctor, whose 42 points in this game continued his personal scoring splurge against the Kentucky club. In the two previous meetings of the teams, Dr. J had racked up 44 and 40, and the combination of Brown's shouting and his team's stop-Erving defense didn't faze him one bit.

"Sure, I heard Brown every once in a while," Julius said later, "but he doesn't mean anything by it. He's just saying those things to psych up his team. Kevin does the same thing with us."

Regarding his sterling performance against the Colonels, Julius said, "Every player in the league does well against some team. I guess my bag is the Colonels. Besides, you can't get up for all eighty-four games, so I try to hype myself up for the big ones. I'm a pro, and that's expected of me. But don't let statistics fool you—there was more than Julius Erving out there tonight. This was a big team victory."

But it was Erving, the hard-court general, who showed his troops the way. One of basketball's most astute and knowledgeable critics, sportswriter Leonard Koppett, wrote:

For total versatility, body control, shooting ability, feeding skill, quickness and strength in a 6'6" package, Erving is beyond anyone I've ever seen. He plays defense and rebounds with the best, too. Add to that all the admirable qualities that get lumped under words like leadership, poise, response to pressure, and consistency, and you approach perfection. He happens to be an exceptionally sensitive, intelligent and decent fellow, too, which doesn't do any harm.

Oscar Robertson and Elgin Baylor usually have been singled out as the most talented "complete" players. Erving, from what I've seen, can do everything they did, and he's bigger. What's more, he has certain flying moves around the basket that I've never seen anyone make—and he does them naturally, as part of the right way to make a particular play, not just effect.

So, if you like basketball, and you get a chance to see Dr. J. in action, go. Television may or may not give you the full dimension of how exciting he can be, but seeing him in person certainly will. Go—and enjoy.

Dr. J really lived up to his reputation in a game played on February 15, 1975. His jump shots were on target; his foul-line-to-hoop floaters were plunking in; his dunk shots were smashing through the netting. His springy legs, big hands, and split-second timing were serving him faithfully on rebounds. And he was also unselfishly feeding off for assists.

Julius—and the Nets—needed to play that well because they were trying to cool off a fired-up San Diego squad on the Conquistadors' home court. The game was tied after four periods. . .after five. . .after six. . .after seven. Finally, after the fourth overtime period, two totally exhausted teams dragged themselves off the floor. The scoreboard showed San Diego had outlasted the Nets, 176–166, in the longest official game ever played. It lasted one hour and eight minutes of actual playing time, and the two-team total of 342 points was also an all-time high. For Julius, who put in sixty-six of the sixty-eight minutes, it produced a career best of 63 points, to go with his 25 rebounds and 8 assists.

The loss didn't do anything for the Nets' ego, and the game itself was a hardship on the Doctors' knees. "It was kind of frustrating," Julius admitted in the losers' locker room, "to play such a long game, put so much into it, and then come out on the short end. There was no real satisfaction to be gained from it. All we had to show for the game was sore feet."

At the end of the season the Nets and Kentucky Colonels crossed the finish line together, tied for first place with identical 58–26 records. A tie-breaking one-game play-off was staged, and the Nets' domination of their archenemies ended as the Colonels won the division title, 108–99.

That defeat, after a long, wearying season, seemed to take the heart out of the New Yorkers. Instead of repeating their play-off heroics of 1974, Loughery's team fell to the Spirits of St. Louis, four games to one. The Nets were dispirited and shocked by the completely unexpected upset, and their glum reaction to being eliminated was voiced by Larry Kenon, who slumped in front of his locker and said, "I can't believe it." There was nothing more to say.

There was a sadness in New York, a city used to its share of championships. Neither the Nets nor the NBA's Knicks had come home with a title. But in the midst of all the gloom there was a shining ray of light, and naturally it was supplied by Dr. J. Although he had ended up second to George McGinnis in the scoring race, with a 27.8 average to McGinnis' 29.7 mark, Julius' fans could point out how well he had played the all-round game. He was the league's sixth best in 3-point shot-making; eighth best in rebounding (10.8 a game); tied for fifth in assists (5.5 a game); fourth in blocked shots (1.8 a game); and fourth in steals (2.2 a game). The complete player!

Nothing could really substitute for the lost championship, but Julius perked up when he was personally rewarded with two awards. First, *The Sporting News* poll of ABA players named him the league's

Most Valuable Player for the second successive year. Then the sportswriters and broadcasters designated him cowinner, with George McGinnis, in their selection of the ABA's MVP.

After learning of the second award, Dr. J said, "It's a great honor to again be chosen and to share the MVP award with a player the caliber of George." It made Julius the second ABA player to win the award more than once, and he looked forward to many more seasons in which to break that record.

There was, however, one problem confronting Julius as he geared up for the 1975-76 campaign. The financial woes and other worries that had plagued the ABA ever since its birth were growing worse. In fact, it appeared that this might be the last season for the league. And, if that turned out to be true, it would also be the last season for the fabulous Dr. J to win another MVP award in the ABA—the one that would make him the league's only three-time winner.

He went after it right from the opening week of play. Like a starving lion on the trail of a meal, he stalked the hardboard jungle, using his incomparable talents, experience and bottomless imagination to elude every snare his rivals set to stop him.

After the 84-game schedule was over, Julius had established himself once again as *the* super-superstar. Scoring? His name was right at the top, with an average of 29.3 points a game. Rebounding? Number five in the ABA, with an average of better than 11 caroms a contest. He was also among the top ten in two-point and three-point shooting percentage, in assists and blocked shots. And, to round things off, he grabbed second place in the steals derby, with 207. That, as ballplayers say, was "doing it all."

If any foolish fans thought Dr. J had done it all and was going to let up in the post-season playoffs, he convinced them otherwise. In the course of leading the Nets to another league title by defeating the Denver Nuggets in the championship series, the great Doctor swooshed and swished, dunked and rebounded, fed his teammates, and directed the floor action with unique flair and intelligence.

Talking of basketball's priceless package of playing perfection, Nets coach Kevin Loughery said, "You know, I'm pretty fortunate that I'm coaching the best basketball player in the history of the game.

"I've never seen a guy, except maybe Bill Russell, who's admired so much by the other players as Doc is. Everyone respects him. In my three years with the team, this has been Doc's best season." Loughery then talked of trades that didn't work out for the Nets, of injuries over the season, and concluded, "so Doc just picked up his game a few notches to pick up the slack. I don't know how he did it. I guess the great ones can do that. In my opinion, I can't see anybody getting the MVP award over him."

Seconding Loughery's opinion was David Thompson, Denver's Rookie of the Year. "There's no doubt that Julius is the greatest," Thompson said. "He's my idol. Maybe I can be to basketball, some day, what Dr. J is today."

What Loughery, Thompson, and thousands of others were remembering was how Julius had come through again and again and again. In the battle for the league crown, Julius swept the boards clean (14.1 rebounds a game); he scored at a clip that averaged out to 37.6 points per game; he stole the ball, blocked shots, upset the Nuggets' offense . . . everything an MVP is expected to do. So, fittingly, he was once more named the ABA's most valuable player—the only three-time winner of that honor.

"I really wanted this one," Julius said at the awards ceremony, leading those who were present to agree that he must feel certain that 1975-76 had been the ABA's last season; that finally the Nets and other ABA teams would be playing against NBA teams; that the ABA would no longer exist as a separate entity. And everyone also agreed that he had wound up this phase of his career in a starburst of glory.

Phase Two—Dr. J and the NBA—offered more honors to pursue, bigger and better challenges, and the chance to be recognized, once and for all, as the best basketball player ever to play in any league.

How many more records Dr. J would break and set was anybody's guess as he got ready for the next season. But everyone associated with basketball was sure that there was no need to guess when it came to picking the one player who belonged on the all-time, all-pro All-Star team. For total ability, for pure excitement, for game-after-game inspiration, absolutely no other player could compare to the marvelous, magical, super-superstar known as Dr. J.!

Index

The Author

Louis Sabin is the author of numerous books and articles. His two most recent books for Putnam's are *Walt Frazier: No. 1 Guard of the NBA* and *Pro Basketball's Greatest: Selected All-Star Offensive and Defensive Teams*. Mr. Sabin, his wife, Francene, and their son, Keith, make their home in Milltown, New Jersey.